# Mrs Ockleton's Rainbow Kite and Other Tales

## THINKING THROUGH LITERATURE

Teacher Resource Book

# Mrs Ockleton's Rainbow Kite and Other Tales

## THINKING THROUGH LITERATURE

Teacher Resource Book

**Garry Burnett**

Crown House Publishing Limited
www.crownhouse.co.uk

First published by

Crown House Publishing Ltd
Crown Buildings, Bancyfelin, Carmarthen, Wales, SA33 5ND, UK
www.crownhouse.co.uk

and

Crown House Publishing Company LLC
4 Berkeley Street, 1st Floor, Norwalk, CT 06850, USA
www.CHPUS.com

© Garry Burnett 2006

The right of Garry Burnett to be identified as the author of this work has been asserted by him in accordance with the Copyright, Designs and Patents Act 1988.

All rights reserved. The purchase of this book entitles the individual teacher to photocopy stories and activities for use in the classroom. The reproduction of any part for an entire school or school system or for commercial use is strictly prohibited. Except as permitted under current legislation no part of this work may be stored in a retrieval system, published, performed in public, adapted, broadcast, transmitted, recorded or reproduced in any form or by any means, without the prior permission of the copyright owners. Enquiries should be addressed to Crown House Publishing Limited.

**British Library of Cataloguing-in-Publication Data**
A catalogue entry for this book is available from the British Library.

10-digit ISBN 1904424422
13-digit ISBN 978-190442442-0

LCCN 2005937425

The poem 'Broken Roots' on page 89 is used with permission from *Urban Gorilla* by Wes Magee (Leeds University Press, 1980. ©Wes Magee).
The music on the accompanying CD is adapted and used with permission from 'Kaz', 'On Camber Sands' and 'Rainbow Kites' from Gordon Giltrap's *Troubador* album (Books Music, 1998 © Gordon Giltrap).

Text illustrations: Les Evans Cartoons & Illustrations, Swansea
Kite illustration on cover: Jeff Turner, STD Musical Services, Hull
Text design: Paul Barrett Book Production, Cambridge
Typesetting: Marie Doherty, Cosham, Portsmouth
CD recording and mastering: Jeff Turner, STD Musical Services, Hull
CD manufacturing: Lemon Media Ltd, Weston-Super-Mare, Somerset

Printed and bound in the UK by
*Cromwell Press, Trowbridge, Wiltshire*

The author and publisher gratefully acknowledge the permission granted to reproduce the copyright material in this book.

Every effort has been made to trace copyright holders and to obtain their permission for the use of copyright material. The publisher apologises for any errors or omissions and would be grateful if notified of any corrections that should be incorporated in future reprints or editions of this book.

# Contents

Acknowledgements *vi*
Introduction *vii*
References to the National Curriculum for English *viii*
Thinking Skills *ix*

SECTION 1 **Stories, Teachers' Notes and Activities Relating to Stories**

Foreword: Music and Stories *by Gordon Giltrap* 2
Introduction to the Stories *by Peter Thomas* 3

1 A Yuletide Tale *4*
2 Mr Gorman *16*
3 Filthy Lucre *26*
4 Uncle Kevin *40*
5 The Man in Black *47*
6 Egging *53*
7 The Mariner's Tale *65*
8 Twenty-six Baboons *74*
9 Billy the Cat *79*
10 Mrs Ockleton's Rainbow Kite *95*

SECTION 2 **Further Guidelines**

11 Multiple Intelligence Approaches to Reading Texts (MIARTS) *110*
12 Anderson's Revised Taxonomy *115*

The icon shown here indicates the stories that can be found on the audio CD accompanying this book.

**Track list for accompanying CD**
1 A Yuletide Tale
2 The Man in Black
3 Filthy Lucre
4 Twenty-six Baboons
5 Mrs Ockleton's Rainbow Kite

# Acknowledgements

I am hugely indebted to my friend Wendy Orr for her contributions and suggestions for activities. Her intelligent and encouraging observations have been at times a revelation and I look forward very much to working on my next project with her. I sincerely hope that some of the joy I have had writing and telling these stories has been communicated here and that at the very least the stories will 'make the reader think'.

And finally ...

I once heard the late great Sir Peter Ustinov, the most child-like and brilliant storyteller I have ever heard, say that he considered the most civilised sound he could imagine to be 'the laughter of a child'.

And that has been, and always will be, my greatest motivation.

Garry Burnett
September 2005

# Introduction

*Mrs Ockleton's Rainbow Kite and Other Tales: Thinking Through Literature* is an English resource primarily written for teachers of students aged 11–14, i.e. Key Stage 3. The stories and their accompanying activities deal with a wide variety of themes, including emotional intelligence, death and bereavement, bullying, friendship, family relationships and growing up.

The activities and assignments are designed to enhance the development of thinking skills and intelligence using texts as a basis and to draw upon original stories, poems, newspaper extracts etc in order to deliver this.

At the beginning of each section introducing the activities that accompany the stories is a series of teacher's notes that give insights into and suggestions for how the stories could be used. They also give details of clear and specific links to the Key Stage 3 Literacy Strategy and relevant Thinking Skills and English National Curriculum levels.

Underpinning the activities is the tireless quest to raise standards of attainment in critical and creative thinking. When constructing tasks for developing responses to each of the stories the questions and activities were partly drawn from an understanding of the following hierarchy of skills developed by Lorin Anderson in *A Taxonomy for Learning, Teaching, and Assessing: A Revision of Bloom's Taxonomy of Educational Objectives* (2001, Allyn & Bacon):

1 Remembering
2 Understanding
3 Applying
4 Analysing
5 Evaluating
6 Creating.

They hopefully reflect the increasingly sophisticated demands suggested by the taxonomy and work by 'step' to create a progressively more challenging reading of the stories. For further details of the taxonomy see page 115.

There has also been a conscious attempt to introduce activities based on the model of multiple intelligences proposed by the celebrated Harvard psychologist Howard Gardner. Gardner's work since *Frames of Mind* (1983, Basic Books) has been to expand our understanding of intelligence by proposing nine (and there could be more) areas of talent and predisposition. Human beings, he claims, have developed 'multiple' intelligences to enable them to solve problems and to represent the world around them, with talents ranging from the following domains:

- linguistic
- logical
- visual
- musical
- interpersonal
- intrapersonal
- existential
- physical
- naturalist.

To concentrate too heavily on one mode, Gardner claims, is to limit the individual's potential or possibly even neglect ways of differentiating material to students that might hitherto have remained inaccessible. A healthy intellectual development, he concludes, will include the cultivation of all of the intelligences and not stereotype children into being a particular learner 'type'.

Further details of how teachers can use Multiple Intelligence Approaches to Reading Texts (MIARTS) with any story or text-based activity can be found in Section 2, pages 110–114.

# References to the National Curriculum for English

The activities that accompany the stories in *Mrs Ockleton's Rainbow Kite and Other Tales* can also contribute to the delivery of the following Key Stage 3 National Curriculum for English levels.

## En1 (Speaking and Listening)

Pupils will have opportunities to demonstrate speaking and listening skills at the following levels:

### At level 5a

a  To match talk to different situations
b  Use vocabulary precisely and organise communication clearly
c  Contribute, evaluate others' ideas, vary participation

## En 2 (Reading)

Pupils will have opportunities to demonstrate reading skills at the following levels:

### At level 5a

a  To show understanding
   Develop inference
   Select appropriate evidence
b  Identify key features, themes and characters
c  Pick out supportive evidence, quotes to support a point of view
d  Understand how texts are organised (and use similar organisational strategies in own work)
e  Compare and contrast texts
f  Discuss the degree of success the author has achieved literary objectives

### At level 6a

g  Read and discuss a wide range of texts
h  Identify *layers* of meaning
i  Identify the effects and significance of texts
j  Express a personal response to texts with reference to language, structure and themes

### At level 7a

k  Select and synthesise information

## En3 (Writing)

Pupils will have opportunities to demonstrate writing skills at the following levels:

### At level 6a

a  To write to engage the reader's interest
b  To use appropriate form and structure

### At level 7a

c  Show clear sense of purpose and audience
d  Express a clear and coherent point of view
e  Write confidently using a range of sentence structures

In the teacher's notes section immediately preceding the activities there are references to the above levels.

# Thinking Skills

The following guide to thinking skills in the National Literacy Strategy is adapted from the DfES Leading in Learning programme. The thinking skills are organised under the following headings:

- Information Processing
- Reasoning
- Enquiry
- Creative Thinking
- Evaluation.

Through speaking and listening, reading, and writing activities relating to *Mrs Ockleton's Rainbow Kite and Other Tales* students will have the opportunity to exercise and develop these important thinking skills. Whereas the activities can be seen as integral to an English programme, they are clearly transferable into thinking and learning contexts across the curriculum.

The references 'S&L' for speaking and listening, 'Wr' for writing ('Wd' for word level, 'Sn' for sentence) or 'R' for reading denote the main emphasis of the activity.

A key to the references for the stories are as follows:

| | |
|---|---|
| YT | (*A Yuletide Tale*) |
| MrG | (*Mr Gorman*) |
| MiB | (*The Man in Black*) |
| UK | (*Uncle Kevin*) |
| FLuc | (*Filthy Lucre*) |
| Mar | (*The Mariner's Tale*) |
| Egging | (*Egging*) |
| 26 | (*Twenty-six Baboons*) |
| Billy | (*Billy the Cat*) |
| MrsO | (*Mrs Ockleton's Rainbow Kite*) |

## Year 7

### Information Processing

| | | |
|---|---|---|
| Wr19 | collect, select and assemble ideas in a suitable planning format, e.g. flow chart, list, star chart | FLuc Billy Egging |
| Wr8 | explain a process logically, highlighting the links between cause and effect | MrG FLuc |
| Wr11 | organise texts in ways appropriate to their content, e.g. by chronology, priority, comparison, and signpost this clearly to the reader | YT FLuc |
| S&L8 | listen for and recall the main messages of a talk, reading or television programme, and record these systematically using abbreviation | MiB 26 |
| S&L13 | compare different points of view that have been expressed, and identify underlying differences and similarities | MiB Billy |

## Reasoning

| R8 | infer and deduce meanings using evidence in the text, identifying where and how meanings are implied | YT<br>MrG<br>MiB<br>UK<br>FLuc<br>Billy<br>Mar<br>Egging<br>MrsO |
|---|---|---|
| Wr13 | express and develop a personal view with clarity | MrG<br>MiB<br>FLuc<br>Billy<br>MrsO |
| Wr16 | use a range of strategies to validate an argument, e.g. statistical evidence, exemplification, testimony | YT<br>MrG<br>MiB<br>UK<br>FLuc<br>Billy<br>Mar<br>Egging<br>26<br>MrsO |
| S&L4 | give a rehearsed talk, which is clearly spoken, helpfully introduced, structured in clear sections and has a convincing conclusion | Mar |
| S&L3 | promote, justify or defend a point of view using supporting evidence, example and illustration, all of which are linked back to the main argument | MrG<br>MiB<br>FLuc<br>Mar<br>Egging<br>MrsO |

## Enquiry

| R1 | use effective strategies to locate and appraise relevant resources for a given task, and find relevant information in them | MrG<br>MiB<br>Billy |
|---|---|---|
| R3 | make brief, clearly organised notes of key points for later retrieval | FLuc<br>Billy |
| S&L7 | use talk as a tool for clarifying complex ideas e.g. by articulating problems | YT<br>Mar<br>26 |
| S&L16 | work together logically and methodically to solve problems and make deductions, test and evaluate the ideas proposed | Mar |

THINKING SKILLS

## Creative Thinking

| R6 | adopt an active reading approach: visualising, predicting, empathising, bringing one's own experience to bear, questioning the text and searching for sense and meaning | MrG MiB UK FLuc Billy MrsO |
|---|---|---|
| Wr5 | experiment with the visual and sound effects of language, including the use of imagery, alliteration, rhythm, rhyme, etc. | YT FLuc Billy Egging 26 MrsO |
| Wr6 | use writing to explore and develop ideas, e.g. journals, brainstorming techniques and mental mapping activities | MiB FLuc Billy |
| S&L15 | use exploratory, hypothetical and speculative talk as a way of researching ideas and expanding thinking | FLuc Billy Mar |
| S&L20 | explore in role a variety of situations and texts or respond to stimuli; reflect on the insight this provides into the motives and perspectives of others | YT FLuc Billy Mar Egging 26 |
| S&L25 | develop strategies for anticipating, visualising and problem-solving in different learning contexts | YT FLuc Mar Egging MrsO |

## Evaluation

| R4 | evaluate the relevance, validity and reliability of information found | MrG Mar MrsO |
|---|---|---|
| R13 | develop critical reflection and personal response, e.g. sharing views, keeping a reading journal | Egging MrsO |
| R14 | review the content, strengths and weaknesses of a text and give a considered response to it | FLuc Mar MrsO |
| WR18 | understand and use correctly terms of qualification, e.g. fully, slightly, similarly, mostly, and of comparison, e.g. less, fewer, more, most, …er/est | UK |
| Wr17 | identify criteria for evaluating a particular text, object or event, present findings fairly and give a personal view | UK Billy 26 |
| Wr21 | find ways of testing the quality of written work, e.g. by using it with its target audience, and refine it in the light of feedback | MiB FLuc Billy 26 |
| S&L12 | reflect on what has been heard to ask searching questions, make pertinent comments or challenge the views expressed | FLuc Egging MrsO |
| S&L17 | acknowledge other people's views, justifying one's own and modifying them in the light of what others say | YT Billy |
| S&L19 | reflect on the effectiveness of the group work and agree how it could be improved | Billy Mar |

# Year 8

## Information Processing

| R1 | experiment with different kinds of note-taking and note-making, choosing a form which suits the purpose, e.g. diagrammatic notes, taking notes during a video, abbreviating for speed and ease of retrieval | FLuc Egging |
|---|---|---|
| R3 | extract and combine relevant information from a diverse range of sources for specific purposes | FLuc Billy |
| Wr7 | organise and present information, selecting appropriate material and making effective use of language, layout and illustration, e.g. a technological process | Billy Egging 26 |
| S&L7 | listen for a specific purpose, paying sustained attention and selecting for comment only that which is relevant to the agreed focus | 26 MrsO |

## Reasoning

| R2 | summarise information or ideas by selecting, generalizing and editing | YT MrsO |
|---|---|---|
| R9 | identify bias and objectivity and distinguish between fact, opinion and assertion | Billy Mar MrsO |
| Wr10 | articulate abstract ideas or emotions for specified groups of readers, e.g. complex feelings, unfolding responses, principles | YT FLuc Mar Egging MrsO |
| Wr13 | present a counterargument to a view that has been expressed, addressing weaknesses in the argument and offering alternatives | YT Egging MrsO |
| S&L18 | use talk to question, hypothesise, speculate, solve problems and develop thinking about complex issues and ideas | YT FLuc Mar Egging |

THINKING SKILLS

## Enquiry

| R4 | undertake independent research using a range of reading strategies, applying their knowledge of how texts and databases are organised and acknowledging sources | FLuc Billy Egging MrsO |
|---|---|---|
| Wr20 | experiment with different approaches to planning, drafting, checking and revising, judging their suitability for the task in hand | FLuc Billy MrsO |
| S&L11 | take the presenter's perspective and techniques into account when interpreting a radio or a television programme | Billy Mar MrsO |

## Creative Thinking

| R5 | review their developing skills as critical readers who search for meaning using a range of reading strategies | FLuc Billy Mar Egging MrsO |
|---|---|---|
| R18 | explore how and why writers exploit or stretch conventions, e.g. to create humour, to surprise the reader | FLuc Billy MrsO 26 |
| Wr1 | use language experimentally to explore ideas, emotions and imaginative experience | YT MrG MiB UK FLuc Billy Mar Egging 26 MrsO |
| Wr 6 | explore the visual and sound effects of language in a variety of poetic styles | YT FLuc Billy Mar Egging 26 MrsO |
| S&L16 | recognise and build on other people's contributions, and find ways of accommodating their ideas in the developing discussion | YT UK FLuc Billy Mar Egging 26 MrsO |

THINKING SKILLS

## Year 9

### Evaluation

| | | |
|---|---|---|
| R13 | discuss their recent reading, re-affirming or revising impressions and opinions in response to the views of others | FLuc Mar |
| Wr17 | evaluate a process or product in relation to agreed criteria, e.g. a design process in technology | MrsO |
| Wr23 | re-read work to anticipate the effect on the reader and revise style and structure, as well as accuracy, with this in mind | YT FLuc 26 MrsO |
| S&L1 | reflect on the development of their abilities as speakers in a range of different contexts and identify areas for improvement | 26 |
| S&L19 | reflect on their individual strengths as contributors to group talk and identify points and opportunities for development | Billy Mar |

### Information Processing

| | | |
|---|---|---|
| R1 | review their own strategies for locating, appraising and extracting relevant information | MrG FLuc MrsO |
| R3 | collate and synthesise information from a range of sources, shaping the material to meet the reader's needs | YT MrG |
| Wr6 | integrate diverse kinds of information into a coherent account, using formal and impersonal language | FLuc |
| Wr18 | plan, organise, edit and present written work effectively, taking account of the time available and the range of possible formats | MrG FLuc |
| S&L4 | recognise what makes a good listener, and reflect on their own skills, strategies and successes as listeners in a variety of contexts | Mar 26 |
| S&L6 | recognise when a speaker is ambiguous, abuses evidence or makes unsubstantiated claims | 26 |

THINKING SKILLS

## Reasoning

| | | |
|---|---|---|
| Wd10 | recognise and use effectively the terms which signpost the development of the line of thought within different types of text, e.g. nonetheless, consequently, furthermore | 26 |
| Wr11 | develop and signpost arguments in ways that make the logic clear to the reader and anticipate responses and objections | Egging 26 |
| Wr17 | record, develop and evaluate ideas through writing, e.g. brainstorming, journals | FLuc Egging MrsO |
| S&L11 | develop critical thinking and problem-solving through questioning, hypothesising, speculating and analysing | YT FLuc Mar |

## Enquiry

| | | |
|---|---|---|
| Sn4 | review their grasp of sentence grammar and the use they make of grammatical knowledge to create and understand texts | YT UK FLuc Billy Egging MrsO |
| R5 | develop note-taking and note-making skills to support analysis and synthesis of what has been heard, read or seen and to help with revision | FLuc Egging |
| Wr18 | plan, organise, edit and present written work effectively, taking account of the time available and the range of possible formats | MrG MiB MrsO |
| Wd6 | know and use the terms that are useful for analysing language effectiveness, e.g. word class, types of phrase of clause, modality, conditional | FLuc Egging MrsO |

## Creative Thinking

| Sn7 | explore the impact of unconventional sentence structures in literary and non-literary texts | YT<br>FLuc<br>Egging<br>MrsO |
|---|---|---|
| Wr1 | entertain the reader by developing an imaginative or unusual treatment of familiar material, e.g. updating traditional tales, manipulating the conventions of story | YT<br>FLuc<br>Billy<br>26<br>MrsO |
| Wr3 | write within the discipline of different poetic forms, identifying how form constrains and contributes to meaning, e.g. different types of couplet or forms of sonnet | YT<br>FLuc<br>MrsO |
| S&L13 | use a range of drama techniques to explore alternative ideas and meanings, e.g. by playing out hypotheses, by changing perspectives | YT<br>MiB<br>FLuc<br>Mar |

## Evaluation

| R4 | evaluate the presentation, reliability and validity of information available through print, ICT and other media sources | Billy<br>26<br>MrsO |
|---|---|---|
| R11 | review their own critical reading skills, habits and experiences, noting strengths and areas for development | Billy |
| Wr14 | cite detailed textual evidence to justify critical judgements about texts and their overall impact | MrG<br>FLuc<br>Egging |
| Wr16 | review their own writing skills to recognise strengths and identify skills for further development | FLuc<br>Mar<br>Egging |
| S&L8 | reflect on the contributions they and others have made to recent discussions, recognising their strengths and identifying areas for development | YT<br>Mar |
| S&L12 | recognise and evaluate the skills and techniques they have developed through drama | MiB<br>FLuc |

In all cases I have tried to give what I consider to be the main emphasis in the selection of activities, in terms of thinking skills, multiple intelligence and connection to the taxonomy of hierarchical objectives. Naturally there will be room for interpretation and the possibility that colleagues will adapt and develop approaches of their own, possibly from the generic MIARTS suggestions in Section 2.

# Stories, Teachers' Notes and Activities Relating to Stories

SECTION 1

# Foreword: Music and Stories

My career as a creative musician started in the mid-1960s with the release of my debut album *Gordon Giltrap* in 1966. This was a mixed affair of songs and guitar solo instrumentals. Between 1966 and 1973 I recorded a further three albums in a similar vein but then decided to pursue an entirely instrumental direction. The result was the critically acclaimed *Visionary* album in 1976. This album was inspired by the poems and paintings of the visionary English genius William Blake. I was particularly moved by three of his most famous poems: *The Ecchoing Green*, *London* and one of his most profound works *The Price of Experience*.

Even though I have written more tunes than I care to remember, the creative process is still a mystery to me and to try to explain how it all works is nigh on impossible. When taking a piece of literature for example as the seed for inspiration, I try to picture what the poem is describing and to put myself in that picture. With Blake of course it's a lot easier, particularly with his more descriptive works such as the aforementioned poems.

I related particularly to Blake and his inherent 'Englishness' and my own style of composing, drawing my inspiration from lute music and the music of Elgar and Vaughn Williams. I can't begin to say whether I hit the mark with some of my interpretations of the masters' works but one can only try to get inside the mind of a tortured genius such as Blake and hope that any scholars of the man will forgive any shortcomings on the composer's part!

I have always been an intuitive creator and this is the only way it works for me. I like to think that in some romantic way that if the man were still alive today that he would approve of an 'intuitive', sincere approach to his beautiful words.

Once the *Visionary* album gained acceptance, it made sense to follow a similar path with the more contemporary work of Harry Willcock and Alan Aldridge, and *The Peacock Party* album was released in 1981. This again was a mixture of text and illustration, a particularly rich source of inspiration for a writer of tunes like myself.

Of course the reverse can also work in the creative process.

The pieces featured behind Garry Burnett's wonderful, innocent, gentle, uplifting story 'Mrs Ockleton's Rainbow Kite' was inspired by music composed for my *Troubador* album. Garry was so moved by my compositions 'Rainbow Kites', 'On Camber Sands' and 'Kaz' that his imagination was fired.

GORDON GILTRAP
June 2005

# Introduction to the Stories

The short story is a subtle form – and more demanding than it may seem at first. Unlike the novel where narrative can uncoil and meander as life does itself, it requires a tight discipline of economical writing. In the short story, everything must be done purposefully – settings established, characters introduced and conclusions worked towards in a very short space. The craft of the storywriter is to invest the little with significance of the large. Garry Burnett's stories have this discipline of condensed material, making them short insights into large human affairs.

Garry grew up and went to school in East Hull and many of his stories draw upon his memories of his family, his neighbours and his classmates. East Hull, however, is not just a geographical setting in these stories. It's true that the landscape of the stories – Holderness Road, the old railway line to Withernsea or the channels of the Humber Estuary – is specifically local but the landscape that really matters is the social landscape of these stories. East Hull is a setting where life is permeated with the culture of its community – the bingo, the chip shop, the 'diddle 'em' and the 'ten-foot' – and these are part of a recognisable wider national culture.

Unlike much autobiographical writing, and unlike much writing that springs from a known community, Garry's work is no rose-spectacled recall of an idealised past. The stories frequently touch on the cruelties of school and family life, as they do with the cruelties of life itself, like the child whose loss of eye and tooth make him doubly handicapped. The stories are in no way a romanticised picture of an urban working-class community. They are sharply realistic and unsentimental.

Many of them draw on the raw and tender parts of childhood – not just pains, but dreams and fantasies, affections and embarrassments. Garry Burnett understands childhood the way few writers do. He understands the way that adults often callously misjudge the needs and hopes of youngsters. The afflicted youth just mentioned, for example, is known to all as 'Dog' because of the inability to even sound his own name 'Doug'. Such unintentional cruelties and ironies outside the politically correct are the distinctive mark of these stories. They are part of the comedy and tragedy of human life. Garry's warmth and affection for characters is intelligent rather than sentimental. He understands that pathos and poignancy are not a matter of emotional wallowing in the agonies of the psyche. His special gift for pathos and poignancy works dangerously close to comedy. Like the great creations of flawed character, Pickwick, Falstaff, Del Trotter or Captain Mainwaring, his characters too are shaped by the absurd collisions of ego and circumstance, of ambition and failure. His Uncle Kevin, in his own eyes a stylish winner in Life's lotteries is, in reality, a walking example of dire failure, but he is sustained against the pain of reality by unperishing self-esteem. There is something of the comic hero about him and others who dare to live their dreams, deaf to the scorn and derision of others, tenaciously holding on to what they want to be whilst driving an ice-cream van whose tune is the theme to Lawrence of Arabia.

What Garry shows us is what Wordsworth knew, that the child is the father of the man. The cruelly handicapped child acts out his dream in the school playground as he pretends to be a bus, zealously developing his repertoire of engine and ticket-collecting vocal effects. In this, he is as one with the chip-shop owner who lives out his dream of being a Confederate General as he doles out skinless haddock or a portion of fries in the 'chippy'.

It's Wordsworth, too, who is the source of so much of what makes these stories more than sketches. In 'Egging', Garry draws on Wordsworth's links between childhood pranks and the dawning awareness of a larger world of conscience and responsibility as two boys hunting eggs are brought suddenly and shockingly to an awareness of matters looming larger than hobbies and pranks.

There are other links a reader may make with writers who have explored the territory of childhood and community – Sid Chaplin, Bill Naughton and Dylan Thomas come quickly to mind. What I think Garry has, uniquely in this collection, is a comic gift for the parochial epic.

My own lasting memory of Garry's stories is his reading of 'Twenty-six Baboons', a story in which the exotic location of a safari collides with the huddle of a chip-shop queue, yoking the lewd vulgarity of the baboons with the disgust of the voyager and the more wildly exotic imagination of the chip-fryer. That and the unforgettable chill of the Christmas story in which a child confronts a mysterious alter-ego. Garry the writer is also Garry the teacher. What he teaches in these stories is warmth, tolerance and the need to dream with our feet on the ground. If he makes you laugh, it's not laughter at individuals or Hull – it's laughter at the quirks and follies of the species.

Thank you Garry.

PETER THOMAS
University of Hull

# 1 A Yuletide Tale

> The day will come when, after harnessing space, the winds, the tides and gravitation, we shall harness for God the energies of love. And on that day, for the second time in the history of the world, we shall have discovered fire.
>
> Pierre Teilhard de Chardin,
> French Paleontologist and Philosopher

You could always tell the kids who'd got new bikes for Christmas because at about a quarter to six on Christmas morning they'd be riding up and down the pavements outside our front window, heaving at their pedals, their bums sticking up in the air like jockeys because the seats weren't quite adjusted to their size yet. Mind you, I was no different. I remember the Christmas I asked for a Raleigh Olympus 'racer'. It was the first big bike I'd ever had and it proved to me at last that I must be really 'grown-up'. All the others I'd had would seem like toys in comparison and for months before I used to daydream about all the places I'd be able to go on *my* new bike.

But then Christmas always began really early in our house and we always used to build up to it by saying things like, 'In two weeks and three days we'll be able to say "It's Christmas this month"' or 'Tomorrow will be the eve of the eve of the eve of the eve of Christmas Eve.' That's what it was like in our house, we couldn't wait for Christmas.

I don't know how our parents managed to give us all they did when money was so tight. 'The good old days?' my Nana used to say, 'They was bad. We had nowt. There were no credit cards or cheque books. We couldn't afford clothes for your Uncle Kevin until he was four, and then we bought him a vest so he could look out of the window.'

I think she was kidding about the last bit.

For six months before Christmas we used to pay a shilling a week into a 'diddle 'em' at my Mum's work. It was our pocket money and a good way, we thought, to save for presents. I always used to wonder why they called it a 'diddle 'em' until one year we didn't get any money because the woman who'd organised it had 'diddled' everyone and spent it on bingo.

When it was finally handed over we would plan our Christmas shopping expedition 'on Road'. It's funny going down Holderness Road for me even now because up to Craven Street not much has really changed. Even 'Aubrey's Discount Super Save', the poor man's 'Fortnum and Mason' where we used to buy most of our Christmas presents, is still there. It contained everything that we needed and (and this was important) at 'affordable' prices. Bath cubes, bath salts, knitted bath salt jar covers that looked like French poodles, Pagan Beast after shave and all sorts of brassy ornaments and paintings of crying children that our aunties and uncles must have been *really grateful* for. The range of presents was endless and it was all 'under one roof'. Do you know one year from my brother I got a packet of Aubrey's Super Save 'Christmas glitter' for a present!

'Oh thank you, it's just what I've always wanted,' I lied.

I wouldn't have minded but he'd used half of it to brighten up the Christmas wrapping paper on the presents he'd bought.

'Oh no, I don't think *he's* been!' my dad shouted up the stairs on Christmas morning as we waited at the top, poised to practically fall down to get to our presents when he'd raked the ashes and lit the fire.

'Oh, hold on, what's this? Come on then.' And we tumbled down the stairs, fighting to get to the spot on the settee or chair where our pile of presents would be.

'Oh wow, look!' said my brother, 'An Adventure Kit. Is the gun real, dad?'

My sister had a doll that could 'wee' and a Junior Hair-Styler beauty salon 'for young models and aspiring film stars' complete with real scissors for styling your doll's hair, hair curlers and make-up.

And there it was, 'six-speed', with gleaming chrome and clean tyres – my racer.

'Can I go out on it, dad?'

'No you can't. It's only a quarter to six and besides you've got no lights.'

Do you remember the films that used to be shown at Christmas? It was different then because there were no videos, and a new film at Christmas was a real event, a treat. After Lesley Crowther had visited the poorly children in the hospital and just before the Queen on Christmas afternoon, I remember one of my favourites being shown that

© 2006 Garry Burnett and Crown House Publishing Ltd – *Mrs Ockleton's Rainbow Kite and Other Tales: Thinking Through Literature*

year, *Lassie*. Lassie was this really clever dog that used to save people when they needed rescuing and she had all sorts of adventures. Actually I think the film this particular Christmas was called *Lassie Come Home* but it didn't matter because they all had practically the same heart-rending story and I would hide behind my comic when the sad violin music began to play, hoping that nobody, especially my dad or Uncle Kevin, would see my eyes fill with tears at the inevitable bit when Lassie nearly died.

'Erhhmm, I'm going to play out on my bike now,' I gulped.

'Ah ha ha ha, look at him he's crying!' my Uncle Kevin shrieked.

'No, no I'm not,' I lied, hurrying outside so I could fiddle with my bike but at the same time sneaking a look through the back window to make sure Lassie was safe. But it was too late, they'd seen me cry now and they soon closed in for the kill, pointing and cackling.

'Get lost!' I shouted. 'I'll run away.'

'On your bike?' said Uncle Kevin. 'Don't you mean you'll ride away?'

'They ought to call you "Lassie",' said my dad. 'Roaring at a film.'

'Here,' said my Uncle Kevin, 'Put one of your sister's dresses on and we'll sit you on the top of the Christmas tree!'

'Right that's it. I'm … going,' I cried, and I slammed the door so hard I thought the glass would fall out.

'Come back, son,' said my mum. 'Take no notice of them. They'll only do it more.'

'They don't care about me! Nobody cares, so I'm going,' and I wheeled my bike angrily to the ten-foot outside, scraping my leg on the pedal as I did. I lingered near the gate, looking around once or twice to see if they'd come for me and say sorry, but they didn't. And once or twice I even thought I saw them waving.

'I'll show them,' I said to myself, tightening the grey, fur-rimmed hood of my khaki parka around my head. 'I won't come back until really late, or maybe even tomorrow, and then they'll worry.'

I pushed uneasily at the pedals as I headed down Telford Street and on to Holderness Road. East Park gates were locked so I turned and headed right, past the cold, empty, closed-up shops and garages out towards Holderness and the open country.

Though my eyes and nose were streaming and my hands chapped red with cold, I didn't stop until I came to Thirtleby Lane, a narrow road between Sproatley and Coniston, at a bend in the lane near a tumble-down barn. I leaned my bike against the hedge and kneeled on the damp grass. And there I sat, all alone on Christmas afternoon with the cold seeping through my black 'sannies' as my breath plumed out in front of me like ghosts.

I looked back at the twinkling lights of the city, yellow and white now against the frosty winter sky as the afternoon began to pink into dusk.

They didn't care that I was on my own. All they cared about was getting drunk and laughing at me.

For a while I just listened.

My pulse thumped gently in my temples from the exertion of the ride. Somewhere across the field crows 'kaa-arked' from twiggy nests that clotted the tops of the bare trees and a ragged robin busied in the autumn debris under the hedgerow.

Just then I thought I heard the faint calling of children as they played in the wood behind me, and it was as I stood up and turned that I saw him. A little boy standing alone at a gap in the wood, garlanded by trees. A small pale boy, lonely at the end of the hedgerow where the fields converged, and he was dressed in exactly the same clothes as me.

I rode quickly now, chased by the gathering darkness back to the lights of the city and my home. Past mud-crusted farms and bungalow front rooms jumping with shadows of televisions and evening fires, until finally I turned into the ten-foot at the back of our house.

'Now where have *you* been?' said my mum softly as I leaned my bike against the wall. 'Come here, I've been so worried about you. Come in and have a warm drink, and some tea. Come on.' And she pressed my damp head gently against her waist.

© 2006 Garry Burnett and Crown House Publishing Ltd – *Mrs Ockleton's Rainbow Kite and Other Tales: Thinking Through Literature*

SECTION 1  **A Yuletide Tale**

I looked through the window at Uncle Kevin and my dad fast asleep on the settee. From where I stood in the darkness it reminded me of one of those crib scenes for the Nativity, though there was something strange about them, and what it was I just couldn't make out.

'I've got something to show you,' she said, holding my hand and leading me through the warm kitchen to the settee where they slept. 'Look at what your sister's done. Won't they know Father Christmas has been when they wake up!'

With her Junior Hair-Styler scissors my sister had virtually scalped Uncle Kevin and my dad as they slept, and in the patchy tufts of hair she hadn't hacked off, she had rolled Junior Hair-Styler curlers, all tightly gripped. They had both been given a full make-over too, complete with eye-liner, blusher and lipstick and sitting on a damp patch on Uncle Kevin's knee, looking like a third ugly sister, was the dolly that couldn't stop weeing, also scalped and with lipstick applied with what looked like marker pen.

I looked down at the three piles of different coloured hair – ginger, brown and bleached blonde – and up at my mum's face and I began to laugh. And as I began to laugh I began to cry, cold shudders of release pulling my shoulders until the Christmas tree lights became genies of liquid colour in my eyes. I was glad I was home. And I knew that it all amounted to what we only ever need at Christmas time, now, and always … love.

## Vocabulary

| | |
|---|---|
| **Parka** | a hooded winter coat, usually khaki in colour and possessing a fur-rimmed hood |
| **Roaring** | slang for 'crying' |
| **Sannies** | cheap training shoes, 'sandshoes' |
| **Ten-foot** | a small alley, an area between houses where garages usually project into and often used by children as a play area – often not more than 'ten-foot' in width |

© 2006 Garry Burnett and Crown House Publishing Ltd – *Mrs Ockleton's Rainbow Kite and Other Tales: Thinking Through Literature*

# 1 A Yuletide Tale

## TEACHERS' NOTES

Pupils will have opportunities to attain at the following Key Stage 3 National Curriculum levels:

### En 2 (Reading)

Pupils will have opportunities to demonstrate reading skills at the following levels:

*At level 5a*

b   Identify key features, themes and characters
d   Understand how texts are organised (and use similar organisational strategies in own work)

*At level 6a*

g   Read and discuss a wide range of texts
h   Identify *layers* of meaning
i   Identify the effects and significance of texts

There is a strong PSHE element to the work included in this unit, most of it dealing with aspects of emotional intelligence. In exploring relationships pupils will develop insights into qualities and skills for impulse control, coping with 'put-downs' and verbal 'bullying'.

The Dylan Thomas 'found' poetry assignment invites pupils to exercise linguistic intelligence through exercises relating to consideration of vocabulary and descriptive prose, as well as exploring features of how texts are organised. Dylan Thomas's work has been an enormous influence on my own, particularly *A Portrait of the Artist as a Young Dog* and his various *Memories of Christmas*.

This particular story was written during a very sad time of personal loss and finished following the death of a close relative and serious illness of another early in December 1995. One Saturday night I couldn't sleep and got up at 3 a.m. to scribble notes and give shape to various ideas I had for a Christmas story. My wife was wrapping Christmas presents and I worked to the wonderfully evocative *A Midnight Clear* CD of Christmas hymn tunes by my good friend Gordon Giltrap. I actually wrote 'A Yuletide Tale' to 'O Come, O Come Emmanuel', and the concluding paragraphs work almost as lyrics written to the rhythm and pattern of that tune.

It was as if writing the story 'surfaced' all the poignant and frustrating emotions of the last few months and when I finished it I just sat and cried. I had never experienced the cathartic release of writing in that way before and as a result I think this has remained a favourite among my own stories ever since.

'A Yuletide Tale' is also available on the audio CD and considering the influence of Gordon's music on my writing, it might be useful to listen to the CD recording in order to reflect on the use of emotional and atmospheric music on this particular track.

⊙ This story can be found on Track 1 of the audio CD accompanying this book.

SECTION 1    **A Yuletide Tale**

# First impressions

Listen to the story carefully and follow the words in your book.

As you listen be prepared to:

- Attempt to 'visualise' scenes from the story 'in your mind's eye'.
- Think about the use of music.
- Discuss your favourite parts of the story.
- Write a list of questions you would like to ask the author in the box below.

Try to answer each other's questions for the author or email them via www.garryburnett.com.

## Discuss (with your group)

- Which were your favourite parts of the story?
- Which parts made you sad?
- How did the boy cope with the verbal bullying by his dad and Uncle Kevin?
- How could he have coped?

© 2006 Garry Burnett and Crown House Publishing Ltd – *Mrs Ockleton's Rainbow Kite and Other Tales: Thinking Through Literature*

**A Yuletide Tale** | SECTION 1

# Impulse control

The boy in the story ran away from home 'on impulse'. This means he didn't really think through what could have happened to him when he did so. 'Acting on impulse' means 'on the spur of the moment', 'without planning'.

### ? Discuss

- What could he have done to cope with the situation?
- Have you ever done anything 'without thinking' that, had you thought about it, you might never have done?
- What kind of 'impulses' do people have that cause them to act without thinking?

### ✎ Write

- Write about a time when someone really lost their temper – it could be you or someone you know.
- Write a letter to a newspaper about something that really makes you angry and that you would like to see changed. For example, bullying, school dinners and so on.
- Make a list of ways of coping with impulses in the box below. For example, counting to ten and so on.

**Top tips for coping with impulsive behaviour**

© 2006 Garry Burnett and Crown House Publishing Ltd – *Mrs Ockleton's Rainbow Kite and Other Tales: Thinking Through Literature*

SECTION 1 | **A Yuletide Tale**

# Put-downs and put-ups

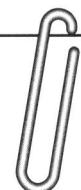

People often give us useful *feedback* on the way we have performed or behaved.

A teacher might write 'That was a good story, but I think you should have more description in the opening paragraphs' on a piece of your writing.

Sometimes, however, feedback can be insensitive and can come across as *personal criticism*.

Sometimes we take criticism badly, even when it is offered with the best of intentions, that is, to help us improve what we are doing.

A good guide is to 'never criticise the person, criticise the act'. For example:

> 'That wasn't a very thoughtful thing you said because …' would sound much better than '**You are** thoughtless' because you are criticising the act, not the person.
>
> *Or*
>
> 'I didn't agree with the way you lost your temper then because …' rather than '**You are** bad tempered'.

People often use personal criticism to put other people 'down', usually in order to put themselves 'up'. Bullying of any kind, including verbal bullying, is something we should not tolerate.

Try doing the following:

- Make your class a 'put-up zone' and design posters that illustrate this.
- Praise someone every day. Make a real effort to congratulate someone on what they have done, on how they look, on something they have said and so on. Avoid saying negative things that put others down.
- Come up with a set of class rules banning certain words and phrases. Try to find ways in your class of 'putting-up' people who have low self-esteem.

© 2006 Garry Burnett and Crown House Publishing Ltd – *Mrs Ockleton's Rainbow Kite and Other Tales: Thinking Through Literature*

**A Yuletide Tale** | SECTION 1

# Optimism

'They didn't love me, nobody loves me.' ('A Yuletide Tale') Isn't it true that when we are angry with people or upset about something, suddenly everything seems bad? Being optimistic and resilient to setbacks is a crucial characteristic of a successful person. In other words they never 'give in'.

Read the following poem by Maya Angelou 'Still I rise'. Maya Angelou has led a remarkable and rich life full of challenges and setbacks, but also full of achievement and excellence. She refuses to ever let anything get her down.

## Still I rise

You may write me down in history
with your bitter twisted lies
You may trod me in the very dirt
But still, like dust, I'll rise

Does my sassiness upset you?
Why are you beset with gloom?
'Cause I walk like I've got oil wells
Pumping in my living room

Just like the moons and like suns
With the certainty of tides
Just like hope springing high
Still I'll rise

Did you want to see me broken?
Bowed head and lowered eyes?
Shoulders falling like teardrops
Weakened by my soulful cries

Does my haughtiness offend you?
Don't take it awful hard
'Cause I laugh like I got goldmines
Diggin' in my back yard

You may shoot me with your words,
You may cut me with your eyes,
You may kill me with your hatefulness
But still, like air, I'll rise

Does my sexiness upset you?
Does it come as a surprise
That I dance like I've got diamonds
At the meeting of my thighs?

Out of the huts of history's shame I rise
Up from a past that's rooted in pain I rise
I'm a black ocean, leaping and wide
Welling and swelling I bear in the tide

Leaving behind nights of terror and fear I rise
Into a daybreak that's wondrously clear I rise
Bringing the gifts that my ancestors gave
I am the dream and the hope of the slave

I rise, I rise, I rise …

Maya Angelou

### ✎ Write

How does Maya Angelou cope with the put-downs and negativity of others?

Choose examples from the poem to illustrate this and her optimism.

# Self-awareness – 'It's OK to cry'

Understanding our emotions is a key feature of emotional intelligence.

Sometimes it's OK to cry and 'get the feelings out'. Sometimes, unfortunately, other people are not sympathetic about other people expressing their emotions.

## Discuss

- Why did the boy in the story 'A Yuletide Tale' want to cry in the first place?
- How did he react to being teased?
- What made the boy in the story feel he couldn't cry?
- How can we be better at allowing people to express their feelings?

## Write

- Write an account of a time when you were so moved or upset by something that you cried.

  **Notes**

- Write a short sketch which includes a situation where you have to show emotional intelligence. Perform it to the rest of the class.

  **Notes**

© 2006 Garry Burnett and Crown House Publishing Ltd – *Mrs Ockleton's Rainbow Kite and Other Tales: Thinking Through Literature*

# Empathy

One of the most effective antidotes for insensitivity is *empathy*, or as Atticus Finch says in *To Kill a Mockingbird* 'putting yourself in someone else's shoes' in order to try to understand how they feel. Show your empathy for the child in 'A Yuletide Tale' by writing him a reply to the following letter as if you were an 'Agony Aunt' (someone who answers personal problems on a problem page in a magazine or newspaper), giving the boy advice on how to cope with similar situations in the future.

> Dear …
>
> I'm fed up of being laughed at by my dad and my uncle. They always seem to pick on me and find things to put me down. What can you advise me to do? I often get so upset I lose my temper and do things on impulse I regret later.
>
> 'Hurt' of Hull

© 2006 Garry Burnett and Crown House Publishing Ltd – *Mrs Ockleton's Rainbow Kite and Other Tales: Thinking Through Literature*

SECTION 1 | **A Yuletide Tale**

# Looking at language: 'found' poetry

One really interesting and fun method of looking at the vocabulary and descriptions a writer uses is to 'find' poetry in their writing. It's really quite easy to do once you get the hang of it and can even help to give you great confidence in your own writing. Here are the stages:

1 Read the extract through.
2 Highlight words and phrases you find interesting or thought provoking.
3 Copy them out on to separate strips of paper.
4 Arrange them into an order you are happy with.
5 Type or handwrite the completed poem, adding in any words and phrases you feel are necessary to complete the poem.

## Extract from *Memories of Christmas*

And I remember that on the afternoon of Christmas day, when the others sat around the fire and told each other that this was nothing, no nothing, to the great snowbound and turkey-proud yule-log-crackling holly-berry-bedizened and kissing-under-the-mistletoe Christmas when *they* were children, I would go out, school-capped and gloved and muffled, with my bright new boots squeaking, into the white world on to the seaward hill to call on Jim and Dan and Jack and to walk with them through the silent snowscape of our town.

We went padding through the streets, leaving huge deep footprints in the snow, on the hidden pavements.

'I bet people'll think there's been hippoes.'
'What would you do if you saw a hippo coming down Terrace Road?'
'I'd go like this, bang! I'd throw him over the railings and roll him down the hill and then I'd tickle him under the ear and he'd wag his tail …'

Bring out the tall tales now that we told by the fire as we roasted chestnuts and the gaslight bubbled low. Ghosts with their heads under their arms trailed their chains and said 'whooo' like owls in the long nights when I dared not look over my shoulder; wild beasts lurked in the cubby-hole under the stairs where the gas-meter ticked. 'Once upon a time,'

Jim said, 'there were three boys, just like us, who got lost in the dark in the snow near Bethesda Chapel, and this is what happened to them …' It was the most dreadful happening I ever heard.

DYLAN THOMAS

## Christmas memory

Sat around the fire
under-the-mistletoe
yule-log-crackling
We told tall tales now
as the gaslight bubbled low

While outside in the white world
padding on the hidden pavements
into the white silent snowscape of our town
Were three boys, just like us,
lost in the dark.

GARRY BURNETT
(with a lot of help from Dylan Thomas)

###  Write

Try it yourself on *Memories of Christmas* and 'A Yuletide Tale'.

© 2006 Garry Burnett and Crown House Publishing Ltd – *Mrs Ockleton's Rainbow Kite and Other Tales: Thinking Through Literature*

# 2  Mr Gorman

> Love is a boy by poets styl'd
> Then spare the rod and spoil the child
>
> SAMUEL BUTLER, *Hudibras*, part ll,
> canto 1, lines 843–4

Mr Padley was our headmaster when I started Southcoates Lane Junior Boys' School and I suppose the best way of describing him would be to say that he was like everybody's grandad. He seemed quite old to me, a boy of eight at the time. The hair had disappeared from the top and back of his head and the sides were always neatly 'brylcreamed' back. He had a chubby pink face and wore thick glasses that can't have worked very well because he didn't seem to be able to see past the first three rows of the assembly hall. It never seemed to bother him if we swayed in time to the hymn or occasionally when Mr Cannon, who played the piano, reminded Whincup, his page turner, to 'get a flaming move on'. In fact I think he found it all quite funny. And now when I try to think of him I get a picture of Captain Mainwaring from *Dad's Army* in my mind and I'm never sure which is which.

But he always made me feel he cared for the boys in his school, as if they were his own – 'his' school. I always thought of it as *his* school, the same way I did my house to be *my* house. For some reason I couldn't imagine him anywhere but there and I was shocked out of my skin to see him eating an ice cream on the promenade at Bridlington one day with his sleeves rolled up. I almost hid in embarrassment.

When our teacher was off 'poorly', Mr Padley would sometimes stand in and take the lesson. He was a wonderful storyteller and had a large repertoire of 'voices' that he would use to bring them to life. Doing plays was best because he would ask 'Who would like to play the part of …?' And before he'd finished everyone's hand would go up. 'No one?' he would then say, feigning astonishment, 'Oh well, I'll have to do that one then.' He would sometimes end up doing every character in the play, each with a different voice, and we would sit back and listen and laugh.

In assembly he would read out articles from the newspaper or tell us about somebody who had had something awful happen to them and we would squeeze our eyes shut while he said a special prayer. I remember well the day of the Aberfan disaster in Wales, when a black mountain of coal debris slipped and engulfed a tiny school, killing many of its children and teachers. Mr Padley stood and dabbed his eyes with his handkerchief as he told us all about it in a special assembly, before reading a poem to remember the dead.

I gave my dinner money to the collection.

So when Mrs Johnston came in one day to tell us that she had some very sad news and that Mr Padley had died unexpectedly during the night, we all felt the loss as though it were a member of our own family. The shiny black funeral cars drove slowly past the school and us boys all lined up on Southcoates Lane to sing 'For Those in Peril on the Sea', the school hymn, joined by hundreds of ex-pupils and parents. I don't think I'd seen so many people gathered in that way until the Queen came to Hull sometime later. There were lots of people crying.

On the first day back at school the following September the floor in the hall shone like glass and the warm smell of varnish and fresh paint made me feel quite faint as we all filed into our first assembly – wearing blazers and haircuts and stiff new shoes. All of a sudden the doors to the stairs burst open and in strode a very serious looking dark-haired man. He stood grimly holding on to the lectern without speaking as he raked the faces of the assembled boys with his glare, pulling down, row by row, the corners of every smile, until there was a hushed gloom in the hall.

'Good morning. Welcome back to the first day of your new term,' he said. 'My name is Mr Gorman and I am your new headmaster.'

Then, without warning, he suddenly pointed and yelled at the top of his voice to a boy in the third row.

'YOU BOY! Yes you. Why is it every time I open my mouth some idiot starts speaking? Anybody who talks when I am has got to be *mental*. Come out here.'

'Sir, I wa'nt honest.'

The boy mounted the stage and Mr Gorman held up what looked like a child's cricket bat with writing all over it. In fact it said 'Heat for the Seat' and there was a little picture of a crying boy with a glowing red bottom who'd just received it.

'Bend over,' commanded Mr Gorman and then he belted the unsuspecting boy on his backside with the bat as if he were hitting him for six.

I remember Borrill, a chubby boy with sticking up ginger hair, being summoned to the front after there was a bit of commotion around him.

'And you are?' he snapped at the quivering boy.

'I am what sir?'

'Don't try to be funny with me. Your name you idiot. What's your name boy?'

'Sir, Borrill.'

'*Sir* Borrill eh? When did you receive your knighthood?'

'Sir, I don't know sir.'

'Well come on boy tell us the joke so we can all enjoy the fun. And since when has "making wind" been a part of the liturgy?'

'Sir?'

Despite being genuinely sorry, Borrill was given two hits from 'Heat for the Seat' and ordered to see a 'vet' for acting in an unholy manner during an act of worship.

When Mr Gorman occasionally took geography classes they were generally unforgettable occasions.

'To the front, Aldridge,' he growled, in the middle of one particular lesson all about the formation of metamorphic rocks. 'You can be my visual aid.'

Mr Gorman took out of his jacket pocket a silver cigarette lighter and flicked it open.

'You will never forget now gentlemen, will you, exactly how metamorphic rocks are formed in the earth? They are formed when there is pressure from above and heat from below. So now, repeat after me ... "Pressure from *above*, heat from *below*".'

As we did so Mr Gorman held the flame of the cigarette lighter menacingly close to Aldridge's chin and pressed down hard with his other hand on the petrified boy's head.

'Pressure from above,' he repeated, scanning our faces and seeming to enjoy our horrified reactions, 'Heat from below.'

If there were ever any complaints from parents about his 'lessons', we certainly never heard them.

We were, it seemed, at the mercy of the beast, and his regime of fear grew as over the next few weeks Mr Gorman bullied us all into a terrified and gloomy silence.

It appeared that everyone was at some stage going to be the focus of his attention and one day after sitting a test to see what grade I would take with me to my new secondary school, I was told by Mr Abram my form tutor that Mr Gorman wished to see me in his office. The loud tick of the school clock was nothing compared to the thumping of my heart in my throat as I lingered outside waiting to go in. I could hear his secretary tapping away at a typewriter in his room. A boy who 'couldn't keep still' in his classroom had been sellotaped by the wrists to the corridor wall. If he moved and broke the tape he had been warned, he would receive 'Heat for the Seat'.

'Come,' yelled Mr Gorman at my feeble knock.

'Sir,' I croaked, 'You wanted to see me.'

'And you are?'

'Burnett, sir.'

'Ah, yes,' he said through thick spectacles that magnified his eyes to menacing proportions and he held up my examination paper in his hand. One of the questions on the paper had been 'Find as many words as you could in "Time"', simply by re-arranging all four letters, and I had written 'MITE, ITEM and EMIT'.

'How would a boy of ten know a word like "emit" if he didn't cheat?' he sneered.

I had recently read a book on UFOs that described the noise a flying saucer had 'emitted' and I'd had to look it up in the dictionary to find out what it meant. But I would swear there was an almost sadistic look of disappointment on his face when I offered this explanation and it made me feel quite sick to see.

He never once said he was sorry.

Late one dark afternoon in February we were called into the hall for a 'special assembly' and nobody dared to look at Mr Gorman as he stared out from the stage at the front of the hall. Bruise-coloured clouds gathered behind him over the

© 2006 Garry Burnett and Crown House Publishing Ltd – *Mrs Ockleton's Rainbow Kite and Other Tales: Thinking Through Literature*

SECTION 1 | **Mr Gorman**

Humber and he stood motionless, silhouetted against the window.

For a long time after we had all arrived he still didn't move.

'Sit,' he said in a menacingly low voice. 'David Meek, remain standing.'

Meek was from a large, poor family. There was, it seemed, a Meek in every year. Some of the boys teased him by calling him 'Meeky Mouse'.

'Right gentlemen,' said Mr Gorman conspiratorially. 'We have before us … a thief. This villain has been caught taking other boys' money from their coat pockets and today I am going to teach him and you a lesson that you'll never forget. Now then lad, put on your spectacles.'

Nobody knew that Meeky should have been wearing spectacles. In those days there wasn't the vast choice of nice frames that you can get nowadays and not many people could have afforded them anyway. You could either look like Buddy Holly or John Lennon and that was it. David Meek, so often the object of scorn for his shabby clothes and shoes, was obviously too proud to endure the jeers of his schoolmates for spectacles and had never once had them on in class.

'I an't gor um wi' me sir.'

'Oh,' said Mr Gorman, feigning surprise, 'It's a good job I went home for them isn't it?' And out of his pocket he drew the boy's spectacles like a conjuror producing the card at the end of a magic trick.

'Come and put them on then,' he snarled, 'And let's see if they're working properly.'

Then he made Meeky face the hymn sheets on the wall.

'And if you don't sing sweetly,' he said, tapping his palm with 'Heat for the Seat', 'I've got something here that might help.'

The clouds over the river could have been foothills of distant mountains or dust clouds scuffed up from stampedes of wild beasts fast approaching as Mr Cannon uneasily struck the introductory chord for 'To be a Pilgrim' and David Meek stood, his face crimson with shame, not making a sound. After the second and third false starts to the hymn, the first tears spilled on to the boy's burning face. He was already broken, humiliated and we all cowered in anticipation of what was to come. The sound he made after he'd received the first stroke was like no other I've heard before or since. After the swift crack of wood on flesh, he 'keeed' in pain, and then again. After the third he collapsed sobbing onto the platform.

I didn't see Mr Gorman for nearly twenty years after I'd left. I was in Sainsbury's supermarket with my little girl. I handed her the shopping and she placed it carefully into the wire compartment at the front before I spun the trolley around like a waltzer car with her inside it. 'Weeee….' she would chuckle before I grabbed the handle to stop it from crashing into the displays.

And suddenly he came around the corner of the aisle, holding on to a trolley himself. He seemed much smaller and thinner than I remembered and judging by the pull on the corner of his mouth he had suffered a stroke and held onto the trolley's handle as if for support.

I felt I should at least show him the courtesy of telling him who I was.

'Oh yes,' he said faintly, not really remembering. 'Weren't you …?' And a thin string of saliva trickled down the side of his mouth. 'Weren't you …?'

I felt like saying 'The boy of ten you were about to beat for cheating because he'd merely taken the trouble to learn a word that he didn't understand. The boy of ten who had stood and watched helplessly while you bullied and intimidated and destroyed the love of learning that was in us all.'

But I couldn't find the words … and neither could he.

How many words can you find in 'time'? How many?

I chilled as he stroked my daughter's chin and then nodded and wished him well. But he died just two weeks later and I saw his obituary in the paper that gave details of how much he had 'left' in estate.

My goodness. For all those who'd been at his many 'lessons', it must seem like he'd left a great deal more.

© 2006 Garry Burnett and Crown House Publishing Ltd – *Mrs Ockleton's Rainbow Kite and Other Tales: Thinking Through Literature*

# 2  Mr Gorman

## TEACHERS' NOTES

Pupils will have opportunities to attain at the following Key Stage 3 National Curriculum levels:

### En 2 (Reading)

Pupils will have opportunities to demonstrate reading skills at the following levels:

#### At level 5a

a  To show understanding
   Develop inference
   Select appropriate evidence
b  Identify key features, themes and characters
c  Pick out supportive evidence, quotes to support a point of view

#### At level 6a

h  Identify *layers* of meaning
i  Identify the effects and significance of texts
j  Express a personal response to texts with reference to language, structure and themes

#### At level 7a

k  Select and synthesise information

I still have the cutting from the local newspaper giving details of Mr Gorman's death. Colleagues who knew him and have read this story since I wrote it said that things were in fact far worse.

The principal activity here is about developing strategies for reading analysis using a systematic approach to 'unpack' questions, though there are also endless potential follow-up activities relating to original writing – for example, school-based experiences – that might be given as well.

The DIAL system is one that could be applied to question assimilation in many other curricular areas in order to avoid contravention of rubric and to focus attention on the requirements of an examination question.

SECTION 1  **Mr Gorman**

# Focus: 'DIAL an answer' (1)

There are many occasions when you might have to 'respond to a text' by answering a series of questions following the close reading of a piece of writing.

In order to read the following passage (from *Charlie and the Chocolate Factory* by Roald Dahl) and the questions that follow, practise using the 'structure' summarised by the mnemonic DIAL. This will help you to understand more effectively what the question requires you to do as you unpick the question.

> Helping to break down reading comprehension questions using 'DIAL'-an-answer.
>
> **D**etails          What will the answer be about?
> **I**nstructions     What do you have to do? List? Compare? Explain?
> **A**llocation       How many marks? How many answers do you have to find?
> **L**ocation         Where will you find the answer? Use highlighter pens.

## Extract from *Charlie and the Chocolate Factory*

*An invitation to take part in a tour of his factory is the prize for anyone who finds a Golden Ticket in one of Willy Wonka's chocolate bars. Poor Charlie Bucket never looks likely to achieve this, his family can barely afford basic food to eat, never mind to buy luxuries like chocolate. So when he finds some money in the gutter, he cannot resist the temptation to buy just one bar of chocolate.*

Charlie went on wolfing the chocolate. He couldn't stop. And in less than half a minute, the whole thing had disappeared down his throat. He was quite out of breath, but he felt marvellously, extraordinarily happy. He reached out a hand to take the change. Then he paused. His eyes were just above the level of the counter. They were staring at the silver coins lying there. The coins were all five-penny pieces. There were nine of them altogether. Surely it wouldn't matter if he spent just one more …

  'I think,' he said quietly, 'I think … I'll have just one more of those chocolate bars. The same kind as before, please.'

  'Why not?' the fat shopkeeper said, reaching behind him again and taking another Whipple-Scrumptious Fudgemallow Delight from the shelf. He laid it on the counter.

  Charlie picked it up and tore off the wrapper … and suddenly … from underneath the wrapper … there came a brilliant flash of gold.

  Charlie's heart stood still.

  'It's a Golden Ticket!' screamed the shopkeeper, leaping about a foot in the air.

  'You've got a Golden Ticket! You've found the last Golden Ticket! Hey, would you believe it. Come and look at this, everybody! The kid's found Wonka's last Golden Ticket! There it is! It's right here in his hands!'

It seemed as though the shopkeeper might be going to have a fit. 'In my shop, too!' he yelled. 'He found it right here in my own little shop! Somebody call the newspapers quick and let them know! Watch out now, sonny! Don't tear it as you unwrap it! That thing's precious!'

ROALD DAHL

© 2006 Garry Burnett and Crown House Publishing Ltd – *Mrs Ockleton's Rainbow Kite and Other Tales: Thinking Through Literature*

# Focus: 'DIAL an answer' (2)

## Practice questions

1. How do we know Charlie enjoyed the 'Wonka' chocolate bar? (5 marks)
2. Compare Charlie's reaction to finding the Golden Ticket to the shopkeeper's. (5 marks)

One of the most common causes of poor exam performance is the failure to read the *question* effectively and therefore to provide the relevant information for the answer. See how DIAL can help that process to be more effective.

## Applying 'DIAL' to an answer

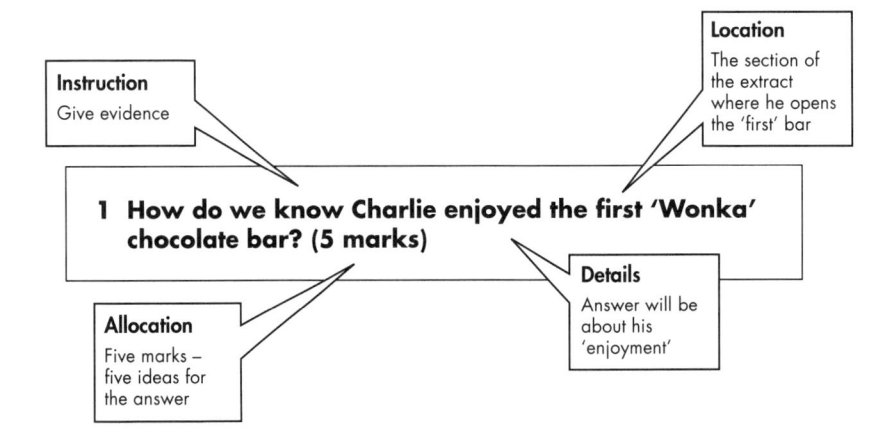

**Instruction**
Give evidence

**Location**
The section of the extract where he opens the 'first' bar

**1 How do we know Charlie enjoyed the first 'Wonka' chocolate bar? (5 marks)**

**Details**
Answer will be about his 'enjoyment'

**Allocation**
Five marks – five ideas for the answer

**D**etails        The answer will include evidence that Charlie enjoyed the chocolate bar.
**I**nstruction    We have to show how we know this is true.
**A**llocation     Five marks means you should try to find five pieces of evidence.
**L**ocation       The section of the extract where Charlie opens the first bar.

## Providing the answer

Now, using a coloured or highlighter pen, go back to the passage and mark five relevant pieces of information which shows us that Charlie enjoyed the chocolate bar. These will form the answer. For example:

- He ate the bar greedily, he 'wolfed' it.
- He didn't pause while eating it.
- He was breathless with excitement and enjoyment.
- He felt 'marvellously happy'.
- He couldn't wait to buy another one.

© 2006 Garry Burnett and Crown House Publishing Ltd – *Mrs Ockleton's Rainbow Kite and Other Tales: Thinking Through Literature*

SECTION 1 | **Mr Gorman**

# Focus:
## 'DIAL an answer' (3)

Now try to apply DIAL to the second question. Write your answers in the boxes below.

**2 Compare Charlie's reaction on finding the Golden Ticket to the shopkeeper's. (5 marks)**

**D**

**I**

**A**

**L**

# Focus: 'DIAL an answer' (4)

Practice these skills on the following passage from 'Mr Gorman'.

Mr Padley was our headmaster when I started Southcoates Lane Junior Boys' School and I suppose the best way of describing him would be to say that he was like everybody's grandad. He seemed quite old to me, a boy of eight, at the time the hair had disappeared from the top and back of his head and the sides were always neatly 'brylcreamed' back. He had a chubby pink face and wore thick glasses that can't have worked very well because he didn't seem to be able to see past the first three rows of the assembly hall. It never seemed to bother him if we swayed in time to the hymn or occasionally when Mr Cannon, who played the piano, reminded Whincup, his page turner, to 'get a flaming move on'. In fact I think he found it all quite funny. And now when I try to think of him I get a picture of Captain Mainwaring from *Dad's Army* in my mind and I'm never sure which is which.

But he always made me feel he cared for the boys in his school, as if they were his own – 'his' school. I always thought of it as *his* school, the same way I did my house to be *my* house. For some reason I couldn't imagine him anywhere but there and I was shocked out of my skin to see him eating an ice cream on the promenade at Bridlington one day with his sleeves rolled up. I almost hid in embarrassment.

When our teacher was off 'poorly', Mr Padley would sometimes stand in and take the lesson. He was a wonderful storyteller and had a large repertoire of 'voices' that he would use to bring them to life. Doing plays was best because he would ask 'Who would like to play the part of …?' And before he'd finished everyone's hand would go up. 'No one?' he would then say, feigning astonishment, 'Oh well, I'll have to do that one then.' He would sometimes end up doing every character in the play, each with a different voice, and we would sit back and listen and laugh.

In assembly he would read out articles from the newspaper or tell us about somebody who had had something awful happen to them and we would squeeze our eyes shut while he said a special prayer. I remember well the day of the Aberfan disaster in Wales, when a black mountain of coal debris slipped and engulfed a tiny school, killing many of its children and teachers. Mr Padley stood and dabbed his eyes with his handkerchief as he told us all about it in a special assembly, before reading a poem to remember the dead. I gave my dinner money to the collection.

So when Mrs Johnston came in one day to tell us that she had some very sad news and that Mr Padley had died unexpectedly during the night, we all felt the loss as though it were a member of our own family. The shiny black funeral cars drove slowly past the school and us boys all lined up on Southcoates Lane to sing 'For Those in Peril on the Sea', the school hymn, joined by hundreds of ex-pupils and parents. I don't think I'd seen so many people gathered in that way until the Queen came to Hull sometime later. There were lots of people crying.

## Focus: 'DIAL an answer' (5)

### ✎ Write

Respond in writing (first apply DIAL). Write your answers in the boxes provided.

**1** Choose three things about Mr Padley that you think the narrator found amusing. Give reasons for your choices. (6 marks)

- 
- 
- 

**2** How do we know Mr Padley was a popular teacher? (8 marks)

- 
- 
- 

**3** Make up three more questions based on the story 'Mr Gorman' in the same style as the ones shown here.

1 _____

2 _____

3 _____

Now swap your questions with someone else in the group and then try to answer them. Don't forget to DIAL first!

© 2006 Garry Burnett and Crown House Publishing Ltd – *Mrs Ockleton's Rainbow Kite and Other Tales: Thinking Through Literature*

**Mr Gorman** | SECTION 1

# 3 Filthy Lucre

SECTION 1 | **Filthy Lucre**

> For attractive lips, speak words of kindness.
> For lovely eyes, seek out the good in people.
> For a slim figure, share your food with the hungry.
> For beautiful hair, let a child run his fingers through it once a day.
> For poise, walk with the knowledge you'll never walk alone.
>
> SAM LEVENSON, American humorist

'Phwoooo, Terry, those socks don't half whiff,' I complained. 'They could probably stand up on their own.'

I'd been camping often enough with my cousin Terry to know that he had the most toxic, smelly feet of anybody I'd ever come across. Sometimes after a hot day's walking or fishing when he 'unpeeled' his shoes from his feet, his socks would almost disintegrate, the sweat was so strong.

'Don't worry, I'll put 'em outside near the food box,' he said. 'It'll keep vermin away from the cornflakes.'

'Aye but what about flies though?' I said. 'They'll think something's rotting and we'll have an infestation. Are you sure you haven't stood in some dog muck?'

But then anything would be better than him leaving his socks inside the tent, where they'd first turn stiff like something that had died and then fill the air with this horrible stink that was like a cross between mouldy fish and stilton cheese.

After a while I didn't so much mind our Terry's sweaty feet. I suppose in a funny sort of way you almost got used to it. It was his sleepwalking that used to really worry me. When he went into one of his sleepwalking trances he would stalk around like Boris Karloff in *The Curse of the Mummy* and he honestly never knew where he was going or what he was doing.

All you usually had to do to stop him was to say in a calm voice, 'Terry, go back to bed now' and that was enough. He went as gentle as a lamb and couldn't remember a thing about it. It was still a bit frightening when we were camping at the Old Mill field in Elvington though and I used to worry in case he would try to go night fishing in the River Derwent and fall in.

We used to talk in the tent until all hours about all sorts of things.

'What would you do if you won the pools?' I asked him once as heavy spots of rain clattered on the fly sheet.

'I'd get our 'ouse done up real nice,' he said as if he'd already planned for this. 'Fitted carpets, central heating an' stone cladding. I'd get a colour telly and take me mam on holiday to Spain.'

'Wouldn't you move?' I asked.

'Why?' he replied.

I remember their tiny little house off Newbridge Road so well. A two-up, two-down, demolished now, like many of the bombed buildings around it, with its tiny creaking kitchen that looked onto a damp, grubby yard where a tin bath hung on the wall next to the outside toilet. There was always this mixed-up smell of Imperial Leather soap, old lard, mice and our Terry's feet and whenever I slept there, sometimes on bingo nights, the purple and orange nylon sheets were never enough to keep me warm. There used to be a coin meter on the stair for the electricity and if it ever ran out when we were on our own, we would be frightened to death to move from the settee, especially when there was no ten pence or foreign coin to put in.

So when this happened we sometimes resorted to cutting up a coin shape out of cardboard, which was fine until the meter man came to empty the box, and then our Terry usually ended up getting into trouble for spending the meter money on something else.

'Are you gormless or what?' said my auntie sending him to bed later with a stinging smack on his bare leg. 'Do that again and I'll really bray you.'

Or sometimes he just didn't think.

'She's hiding upstairs because she's skint and Mr Ladigus the club man is coming,' said our Terry to Mr Ladigus himself, as he peeped through the gap in the net curtain one day.

You don't seem to hear that phrase 'I'll bray you' so much nowadays in Hull, but when I was a boy we seemed to hear it all the time, especially when our Terry was around. You see he always seemed to be getting 'brayed' and often for things my mum would never have bothered with.

And the way I mostly remember him as a boy, he was always running, sometimes to take back

© 2006 Garry Burnett and Crown House Publishing Ltd – *Mrs Ockleton's Rainbow Kite and Other Tales: Thinking Through Literature*

empty lemonade bottles to Alcock's or Martha's for the sixpence deposit or cigarette coupons back to the post office for cash.

'Bring me the change, you Terry,' my auntie would say as he sprinted down Newbridge Road. 'I'll need it for bingo.'

For years my mum and aunties used to go to the Mecca Bingo on Beverley Road. 'We were sweating for a hundred pounds' they would say when they came in. This might not seem a lot nowadays but when you only earned eight or nine pounds a week as a cleaner it really mattered. So when my dad used to say 'Your mam's praying to Mecca' on a Thursday night, we understood what he meant.

Every Sunday in the summer holidays Joe Marrazza, the caretaker at my mum's work, organised a corporation bus trip to Scarborough. It only cost us five pence each and I think that this was to treat the driver who had given up his Sunday especially for us.

'Joe's Trips' we used to call them.

One of the highlights of the trip was the on-board bingo game, and my mum and my many aunties – Sheila, Iris, Sandra, Barbara and Enid (they weren't all really my aunties) – would be upstairs puffing away at their Park Drives while they marked their cards as if their lives depended on it.

'A Wilson's-a-den a number ten,' old Joe would shout, or 'A two and a one a (my age) twenty-one.'

'Get away!' they all babbled.

And so on until the lucky winner would shout out 'Eeyar!' and the main prize of two pounds fifty pence would be handed over in a little blue bank sack.

Sometimes we sang …

'Oh this year we're off to Sunny Spain,
Ee vee var Espanniya
We're taking the Costa Brava plane,
Ee vee var Espanniya'

as we wound our way through Humanby Gap and past Cayton Bay.

*Oh we did love to be beside the seaside …*

… And although it was only 11 o'clock when we arrived, the heat met us as we stepped off the bus to the beach like waves from an opened oven door. Towels became makeshift changing room tents as pink-white bodies wriggled and writhed in various states of dress. Then a dash for the water with lilos and rubber tyres, or collecting scallops in tin buckets for sandcastles with paper flags and plastic windmills.

*Oh we did love to be beside the sea.*

'Here's a pound note, you Terry. Go and get me ten Park Drive and a box of matches,' ordered my Auntie Sheila as we finished our gritty egg sandwiches. 'And don't you go near them amusements with the change. It's all I've got left.'

After ten minutes of waiting, I began to get worried that temptation had probably been too strong. Judging by the way Auntie Sheila kept looking around anxiously, she too was obviously concerned, though more likely for what remained of her last pound note than anything.

'You go find him, you Garry, and tell him that when he gets back here, if he's been in them amusements, I'm gonna bray him.'

A dark cloud had drifted across the sun and for a while the garish colours of the seaside prom were washed with pale grey light. I picked barefoot along the sandy promenade, peering into the seafront arcades and cheap souvenir shops until, in Corrigans, I finally saw him, standing at a fruit machine. He was looking around shiftily, nervously, and when he saw me he beckoned me over, almost pleading.

'Terry, your mam's going mad, she's gonna bray yer.'

'But it won't stop paying out!' he said. And as the barrels spun around and first two lemons and a cherry, then a bell, a melon and a pear and then three plums appeared and out poured a pile of coins without our Terry putting a single penny in the machine.

'It just keeps going,' he said, sounding a bit frightened, and when I looked down his shorts pockets were just full of coins.

'You pretend you're putting something in to make it go,' he said. 'Then maybe they won't think owt's wrong.'

© 2006 Garry Burnett and Crown House Publishing Ltd – *Mrs Ockleton's Rainbow Kite and Other Tales: Thinking Through Literature*

SECTION 1 | **Filthy Lucre**

So for the next twenty-five minutes we just carried on scooping jackpot after jackpot into our shorts pockets until finally the machine coughed itself empty and no more money came out.

Our Terry looked at me and I looked at him as we stepped out into the bright white sunshine on Scarborough promenade. I felt really guilty just standing there, as if we'd been shoplifting or something and at first our Terry could only say one word.

'Yessss,' he said. 'Yessssssssss.'

'She won't "chow" at me when she sees all this will she?' he said. 'We're rich!'

Our pockets looked like huge cowboys' chaps slapping against our legs as we stomped back towards the beach. It's not surprising people kept turning around to look because it was only our Terry's snake belt that kept his shorts from falling completely down his bum, what with all that weight. And judging by the way we were both walking it looked as though we'd had an accident on the way to the toilet.

And as we waddled past the stacked-up lobster pots and crab stalls, the lines of little shops selling pink coral and painted scallops all festooned with kites and nets filled with inflatables and bright beach balls, we heard sea birds chattering over the sirens and bells in crowded arcade halls and bingo bars ringing and chinging and I could see our Terry, chuckling to himself, behind the biggest grin I'd ever seen.

'Oh look, there's your mam,' I pointed out to him.

'Mam! Oh no, mam,' he said in sudden desperation. 'It's not what you think. No mam, listen, you won't bray me when you know.'

'Where the 'ell have you been?' she snarled, clenching her teeth and lifting her hand ready for the attack. Then all of a sudden a transformation came across her face as our Terry held up a huge fistful of ten pence pieces and her head began to rock in a kind of embarrassed apology as she smiled, showing her teeth.

'Good lad' was all she could say, her eyes going wide, 'Good ... lad.'

For the next fifteen minutes Auntie Sheila kneeled to count Terry's money on a large green towel while he sat in a deck-chair looking like 'king for a day', licking a large 99 ice-cream.

'Forty three pounds and seventy pence,' she said eventually with a piggy snort. 'I could have six weeks off work with that.'

I jumped at the sudden blur of movement as our Terry reached to pick up a loose coin on the edge of the towel.

'Get your bloody 'ands off,' she snapped, nearly taking his arm off with a slap. 'You were sent on an errand with my pound note and you spent it. You wanna count yourself lucky you din't get brayed.'

'You mean you're keeping it,' he said, and a little line of milky melted ice-cream ran warm down his chin. 'All? But mam ...'

'No buts ...'

'But ...'

'I said ...'

For a long time after Auntie Sheila had stuffed the money into a carrier bag our Terry sat silent and sulky on his towel, his ice-cream dumped like a tab-end in the sand. I tried to get him to come down to the sea for another paddle, but he just sat staring at the seagulls fussing over bins stuffed with chip trays. I thought for a moment he was going to cry when I saw his bottom lip move, until I heard him mutter something under his breath.

'What did you say?' snarled Auntie Sheila, lifting her head. 'Just you repeat it if you dare.'

All the surrounding beach crowd in their deck-chairs who had watched her count out the fortune on the towel had joined in to listen too.

'Go on,' she dared, pointing to her lips. 'And if you haven't got the guts just keep this shut.'

'Shitty arse,' he said, softly at first and then louder as he sprinted down the beach.

*'Bloody shitty arse!'*

For a chain-smoker my auntie didn't half move fast in pursuit of him and when I heard the slap and the yell a short time later as our Terry was 'brayed', I guessed they must have been at least a quarter of a mile down the beach.

As 5 o'clock came around we all climbed back on the bus and I felt my white cotton T-shirt cool

© 2006 Garry Burnett and Crown House Publishing Ltd – *Mrs Ockleton's Rainbow Kite and Other Tales: Thinking Through Literature*

against my burning shoulders and my hair all stiff with salt and sand. The bus seats, cooked all day by the belting sun, stung against my bare legs as I sat down.

Terry sat quietly as the bus pulled away.

'I'll get you back,' he said, hardly moving his mouth and never once taking his eyes off the enemy. 'You wait and see.'

But the rocking of the bus and the end of the afternoon heat was enough soon to send me deep into dreams. Dreams of trailing kites and swing boats teetering on the brink of summer blue skies, dreams of boys skipping huge foaming breakers on the glazed edge of the sea and a sunset's heavy clouds piled high like gold coins in the sky.

And at my feet, an abandoned ice-cream cornet lies, upturned and still on the beach and all sugar-frosted with sand.

It might have been the sound of retching that actually woke me, or it could have been the combination of disgusting smells that now filled the bottom deck of the bus, but I soon guessed our Terry's feet had something to do with it as he sat with his pumps off watching the aunties fuss around puking children with carriers and tissues.

'Is our Terry playing out?' I asked my auntie when I went around with my mum the next day.

'No love, he's not. He was naughty last night so he's staying in his bedroom for a punishment.'

'Why, what did he do?'

'He came into my bedroom at 3 o'clock this morning,' she said, directing the answer to my mum now as well. 'He frightened our Pete to bloody death. Stood over the bed with a carving knife in his hand. He'd sleepwalked down to the kitchen to get it. If I an't a brayed him, he'd have stuck us both.'

Our Terry told me later it was worth the great smack across his cheek just to see my auntie's face, because he wasn't really sleepwalking at all this time, he just did it to frighten her – you just never would have guessed it at the time.

As I stepped out into the dark condemned terrace to go home, I looked up to see the front net curtain part and his marked face peep out from behind it. In his raised hand he held a pound note – it was the same pound note he had been given the day before for my auntie's errand, and which he had never spent.

And as I stood waiting for my mum, I saw two other boys, also 'serving time', signal to each other from behind twitching nets across the bays.

When I looked up again to our Terry the curtain dropped.

'Time to go now,' whispered my mum, gently. 'Time … to go.'

## Vocabulary

| | |
|---|---|
| **Bray** | to hit, fight, strike |
| **Chow** | complain, reprimand |
| **Club man** | a debt-collector |

© 2006 Garry Burnett and Crown House Publishing Ltd – *Mrs Ockleton's Rainbow Kite and Other Tales: Thinking Through Literature*

# 3 Filthy Lucre
## TEACHERS' NOTES

Pupils will have opportunities to attain at the following Key Stage 3 National Curriculum levels:

### En 2 (Reading)

Pupils will have opportunities to demonstrate reading skills at the following levels:

*At level 5a*

a  To show understanding
   Develop inference
   Select appropriate evidence
b  Identify key features, themes and characters
c  Pick out supportive evidence, quotes to support a point of view

*At level 6a*

j  Express a personal response to texts with reference to language, structure and themes

*At level 7a*

k  Select and synthesise information

### En3 (Writing)

Pupils will have opportunities to demonstrate writing skills at the following levels:

*At level 6a*

a  To write to engage the reader's interest
b  To use appropriate form and structure

*At level 7a*

c  Show clear sense of purpose and audience
e  Write confidently using a range of sentence structures

One of the main activities here, 'My perfect day', is excellent for examining personal *goal orientation*. Wealth fantasy is the central theme of the story and obviously both the story title and Auntie Sheila represent cruel covetousness in the midst of poverty. Children could be challenged to explain how their 'perfect day' reflects their life-goals and whether they are in fact goal-orientated or simply covetous and hedonistic.

The story is based on actual events although the character of Auntie Sheila is very much a caricature of some of the hard-faced characters from an estate close to where I was brought up. Hull has a long sea-faring tradition and one consequence of the men being away for long periods of time on trawlers and merchant ships was that a matriarchal dominance emerged in some communities, leaving a legacy of tough, sometimes harsh, female leaders. Auntie Sheila is a creation drawn from those ranks and nothing like any of my real aunties.

This story can be found on Track 3 of the audio CD accompanying this book.

**Filthy Lucre** | SECTION 1

# Filthy Lucre

1. Before beginning the activities in response to 'Filthy Lucre' take some time to think about your own personal life-goals. What are your main aims in life? How do you hope to achieve them?

2. What do you think the phrase 'filthy lucre' means and why is it an appropriate choice of title for this story?

3. Choose three of your favourite descriptive phrases and words from the story. Illustrate them with colourful and interesting pictures.

4. Make a cartoon comic-strip version of the seaside story.

5. Write Terry's diary for the day of the incident with the fruit machine. Think carefully about his different emotions during the day and how he coped with the reaction of his mother to his behaviour.

6. In your opinion does Terry get 'what he deserves'? Why?

7. Should he have kept the money from the one-armed bandit?

8. Has anything ever happened to you that you thought was 'so unfair'? Describe such a time.

9. Re-read the following description of the seaside from 'Filthy Lucre'.

> And as we waddled past the stacked-up lobster pots and crab stalls, the lines of little shops selling pink coral and painted scallops all festooned with kites and nets filled with inflatables and bright beach balls, we heard sea birds chattering over the sirens and bells in crowded arcade halls and bingo bars ringing and chinging and I could see our Terry, chuckling to himself, behind the biggest grin I'd ever seen.
>
> … But the rocking of the bus and the end of the afternoon heat was enough soon to send me deep into dreams. Dreams of trailing kites and swing boats teetering on the brink of summer blue skies, dreams of boys skipping huge foaming breakers on the glazed edge of the sea and a sunset's heavy clouds piled high like gold coins in the sky.
>
> And at my feet, an abandoned ice-cream cornet lies, upturned and still on the beach and all sugar-frosted with sand.

- Make a visual 'frieze' of 'summer' and 'the seaside'.
- How does the author describe the seaside scene?
- Write your own descriptive account of 'A day at the seaside'.

© 2006 Garry Burnett and Crown House Publishing Ltd – *Mrs Ockleton's Rainbow Kite and Other Tales: Thinking Through Literature*

SECTION 1 | **Filthy Lucre**

# My perfect day

### ✎ Write

Write a story that ends with the line:

**So ended the most perfect day
I could ever have wished for.**

In this story you can imagine anything happening. You can be with anyone you choose, go anywhere, do anything and spend unlimited amounts of money.

The 'day' lasts for 24 hours and can begin at anytime you like (for example, 10 a.m. to 10 a.m.).

### Review: goal orientation

Look back at your responses to question 1 on activity sheet 'Filthy Lucre' and the activity on the left.

- Do they connect?
- Does your perfect day actually include anything that will take you nearer to completing your life-goals?
- Is your perfect day just a day of self-indulgence?
- What does this tell you about your commitment to your life-goals?

# The narrator

A story can become completely different depending on who is telling it and their point of view.

- Who is telling the story?
- What tells us that this story is not set in the present?
- What genre do you think this story is?

### Getting inside the narrator's head

1. What are Terry and the narrator doing at the start of the story? What other activities did they do together?
2. What words show us that the narrator cares about his cousin?
3. What would Terry do if he won the pools and what does this tell us about what's important to him?
4. What tells us that the narrator is surprised by his response?
5. In what ways do you think the narrator is different to Terry in their view of the world? Give reasons.
6. 'I didn't so much mind our Terry's sweaty feet.' What do you think these words tell us about the narrator's relationship with Terry?
7. Who do you think is the elder of the boys? Why?
8. What words tell us that the boys spent a lot of time together?

### Point of view

How would this story be different, if the narrator was:

- Auntie Sheila?
- Terry?
- Joe, the coach driver?

© 2006 Garry Burnett and Crown House Publishing Ltd – *Mrs Ockleton's Rainbow Kite and Other Tales: Thinking Through Literature*

# Hot-seating

As a group, draft a series of interview questions for the characters about who should have the money at the end.

Choose one person in your group to 'be' a particular character from the story.

Take turns 'hot-seating' as a different character. In what ways does the story become different from their point of view?

# Characterisation

| Character | a person in the story |
|---|---|
| Characterisation | everything a writer does in their writing to make a character seem believable and real |

The characterisation of Terry is very vivid. How does the writer achieve this? Let's look at the tricks of the trade, or, the writer's narrative devices.

## Cousin Terry

1  How are we introduced to Terry and why is this an effective start to the story?
2  What does the narrator remember that Terry was 'always' doing?
3  What words show us that Terry is a bit frightened of his mum?
4  How do we know that Terry has a history of spending money he shouldn't?
5  What does Terry do in the middle of the night and why do you think the author mentions this at the beginning of the story?
6  Why did the narrator think that the pound note would be a 'temptation'?

## Auntie Sheila

1  '"Where the 'ell have you been?" she snarled, clenching her teeth and lifting her hand ready for the attack.' What is the author comparing Auntie Sheila to?
2  List all the occasions that Terry gets 'brayed'. What does this tell us about this family relationship?
3  What evidence is there that Terry loves his mum anyway?
4  How do we already know that money is important to Auntie Sheila?
5  Explain the metaphor 'praying to Mecca'. What does the word 'praying' suggest about how important money is?
6  When is the only time that Auntie Sheila is nice to Terry? Describe what she does to reward him.

© 2006 Garry Burnett and Crown House Publishing Ltd – *Mrs Ockleton's Rainbow Kite and Other Tales: Thinking Through Literature*

SECTION 1   **Filthy Lucre**

# Character mind map

How does the author bring a character alive?

- What they do (dialogue)
- What they say (action)
- Qualities
- Relationships

Build a character sketch by adding evidence from the text into your mind map.

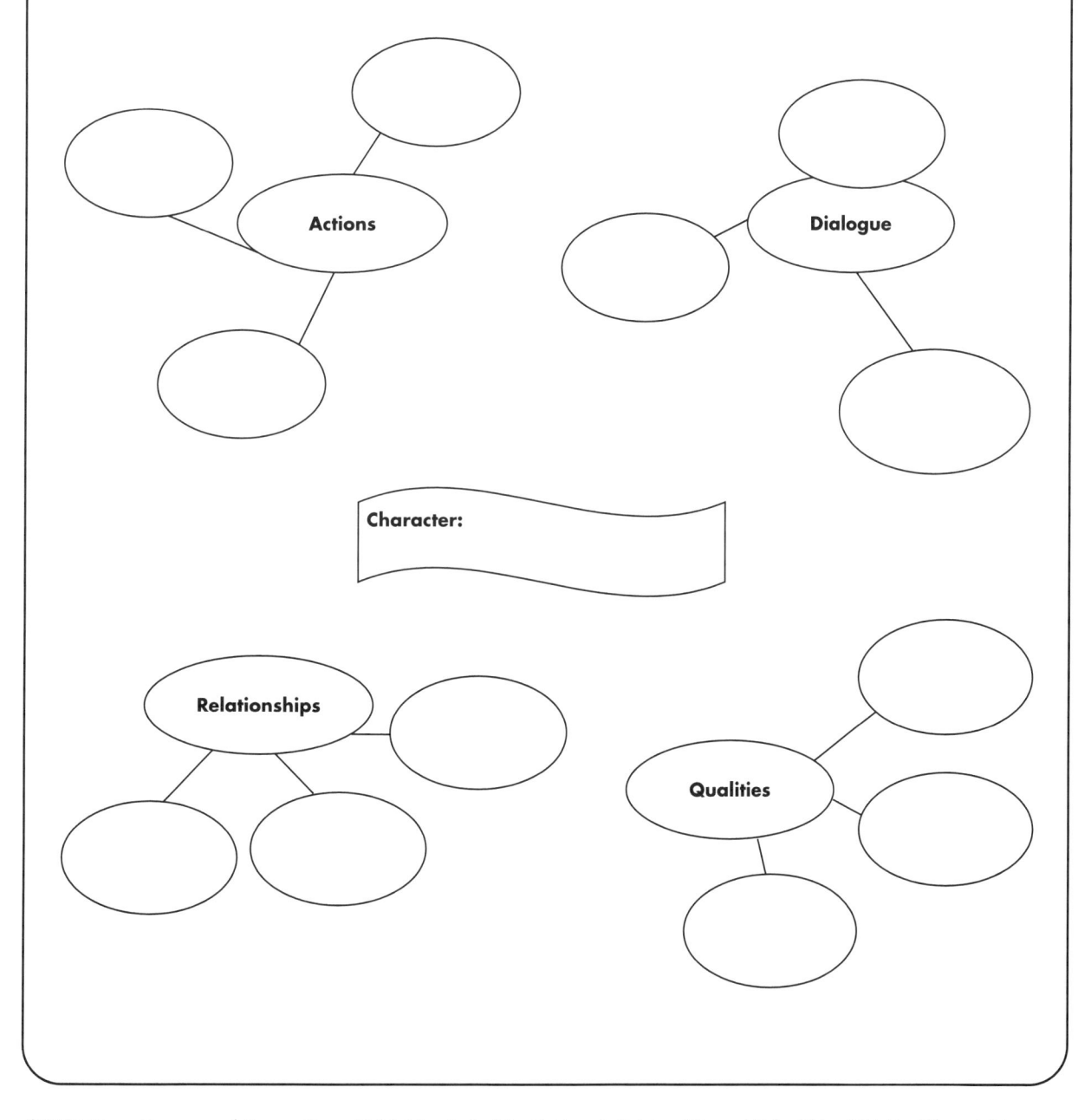

**Actions**

**Dialogue**

**Character:**

**Relationships**

**Qualities**

© 2006 Garry Burnett and Crown House Publishing Ltd – *Mrs Ockleton's Rainbow Kite and Other Tales: Thinking Through Literature*

**Filthy Lucre** | SECTION 1

# Sequencing task

Put these events in the order in which they actually happened. Write the number of the order in the boxes below.

☐ The fruit machine keeps paying out jackpots.

☐ Terry pretends to be sleepwalking.

☐ Auntie Sheila chases Terry down the beach.

☐ Auntie Sheila orders Terry to go to the shops to buy her 'Park Drive' cigarettes and matches.

☐ The narrator complains about Terry's smelly socks.

☐ Terry and Garry return to the beach with bulging pockets full of money.

☐ Some of the passengers are sick on the bus.

# Structure and tone

The narrator varies the tone and mood of the story through placing lively dialogue next to quiet descriptive passages. This contrast creates added drama. The author is playing with structure (the order of the story) to add meaning.

Circle any tone you think is featured in the story:

| angry | sarcastic | reflective | bitter | humorous |
| contented | light-hearted | melancholic | frantic | fearful |

1 *'Oh we did love to be beside the seaside …'* Why are these words in italics?

2 How does the tone change after this line and how does the writer achieve this?

3 Describe how the pace changes in between the italics. How is the storytelling different in this section?

4 The narrator describes the heat 'like waves from an opened oven door'. What does this comparison tell us about the boy's life experience and background?

5 What type of comparison is this?

6 What tells us the people on the beach are not used to sun?

7 'Here's a pound note you Terry'. What does the placing of the word 'you' tell us about the background of the speaker?

8 'A dark cloud had drifted across the sun'. What effect does this image have in contrast to the shouting of Auntie Sheila?

9 What effect does the writer's description of colour and weather have on the tone of the story?

© 2006 Garry Burnett and Crown House Publishing Ltd – *Mrs Ockleton's Rainbow Kite and Other Tales: Thinking Through Literature*

SECTION 1 | **Filthy Lucre**

# Building up tension

Read from 'You mean you're keeping it …' to when they all climb back on the bus for the return journey.

1 How does the author build up tension to create a comic climax?

2 'All the surrounding beach crowd in their deck chairs who had watched her count out the fortune on the towel had joined in to listen too'. What effect does this fact have on the reader as we wait to see what happens next?

3 What else does the writer do to build up the tension as Terry watches his mum count the money?

4 'And if you haven't got the guts just keep this shut'. What is the author doing to build up tension?

5 Which words in this passage show us that Terry is gradually daring to fight back?

6 How does the author highlight how ridiculous it is for Aunt Sheila to be running after Terry?

## Irony

Read from 'As I stepped out into the dark …' to the end.

1 Why is the terrace described as 'condemned'? Who is really condemned?

2 Why is Terry's face described as 'marked'?

3 Why is it ironic that Terry still has the 'same pound note'?

4 What words does the author use in this passage to suggest that the boys are imprisoned?

5 Why are the nets 'twitching'?

6 Why does the story end with the narrator 'looking up' at Terry? Explain what this shows us about the boys' relationship?

7 Why do you think the story ends with Terry alone upstairs and the narrator being led away by his mum? What might it say about growing up and family relationships?

© 2006 Garry Burnett and Crown House Publishing Ltd – *Mrs Ockleton's Rainbow Kite and Other Tales: Thinking Through Literature*

**Filthy Lucre** | SECTION 1

# Imagery: Joe's trips

Brainstorm words/pictures that represent a British trip to the seaside for you:

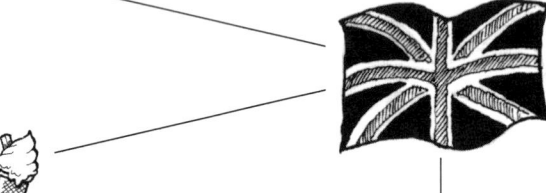

What other images of a seaside trip does the author use in his descriptions throughout the story? Add these in to create a sense of the story's setting.

© 2006 Garry Burnett and Crown House Publishing Ltd – *Mrs Ockleton's Rainbow Kite and Other Tales: Thinking Through Literature*

SECTION 1 | **Filthy Lucre**

# Metaphor and simile

In contrast to the comic tone of the beach chase, the author highlights the narrator's more reflective character.

Read closely this descriptive passage. In pairs, highlight one simile and one metaphor. Discuss the effect of this language.

> But the rocking of the bus and the end of the afternoon heat was enough soon to send me deep into dreams. Dreams of trailing kites and swing boats teetering on the brink of summer blue skies, dreams of boys skipping huge foaming breakers on the glazed edge of the sea and a sunset's heavy clouds piled high like gold coins in the sky.
>
> And at my feet, an abandoned ice-cream cornet lies, upturned and still on the beach and all sugar-frosted with sand.

- What does the upturned cone symbolise in the narrator's dream?

- What other image in this dream highlights something that is very important to Auntie Sheila and Terry?

- What is the author telling us about the narrator's experience by including these images in his dreams?

- How does the author directly contrast the imagery of the narrator's inner thoughts to the more comical exploits of Terry and his family?

© 2006 Garry Burnett and Crown House Publishing Ltd – *Mrs Ockleton's Rainbow Kite and Other Tales: Thinking Through Literature*

**Filthy Lucre** | SECTION 1

# 4 Uncle Kevin

> FESTE  Beshrew the knight's in admirable fooling.
>
> SIR ANDREW  Aye he does it well enough if he be disposed, and so do I too. He does it with better grace, but I do it more natural.
>
> WILLIAM SHAKESPEARE, *Twelfth Night*

'Double or quits?' said my Uncle Kevin as I potted another winning black on my Hurricane Higgins Junior Championship table.

'Come on, you set 'em up.'

Well! Now that would make two hundred and fifty-six pounds he owed me in all and I began to get the feeling that the chances of me actually seeing my winnings were becoming more and more remote.

'Or do you want to lark darts instead?'

You'd never guess he was my mum's brother just to look at him. His podgy, lard-coloured stomach pushed open a gap between his T-shirt, and his half-mast jeans, which revealed at his ankles white 'virgin' socks and black and white baseball boots. Up at the top, a dark mess of ginger hair stood up like a tray of cress above his speckly rounded face and his thin pink lips parted to reveal a beautiful, large, full set of teeth.

I suppose he took the losing so seriously because he couldn't stand what he thought was 'loss of face'. Not that it ever prevented him from trying to show me up at all – in fact I think that was all a part of the game. And it had been like that for as long as I could remember.

Because my nana was too poor to afford a proper holiday, when he was a boy Uncle Kevin nearly always ended up coming away with us to Wallis's Holiday Camp at Cayton Bay near Scarborough. It was a proper 'Hi-de-hi' holiday camp like Butlin's and the week was packed with activities and competitions for kids and parents alike.

The best thing about it for us kids was the 'OK Corral' children's club run by 'Uncle Bernie'. Not only could he organise games and competitions, hypnotise people, tell funny stories and jokes *and* do magic, he could get 200 kids to be completely silent in less than three seconds. All he had to say was:

Sh Sh Sh Sh *Shhhh*

Then, as one, all of the kids would reply '*Sh, Sh*', and immediately put their fingers on their lips. A stroke of genius. Uncle Bernie dressed like Jack Palance in *Shane* and wore a big star made out of silver foil with 'Marshall' written on it. The first and, he said, the most important job he had to do with new arrivals on Saturday nights was to appoint a 'deputy' and because he was a bit bigger and I'm sure a bit dafter looking than the others, this particular year he chose my Uncle Kevin. Uncle Kevin took to the stage as if he'd won the Nobel Prize as Uncle Bernie went through the all-important initiation ceremony with him.

'Repeat these words after me,' he said, winking at the parents with his good eye.

'Uncle Bernie's deputy …'

'Uncle Bernie's deputy …' repeated Uncle Kevin.

'Must not be …'

'Must not be …' echoed Uncle Kevin.

'Half-hearted.'

'Ar farted.'

'You did what deputy? Well stand down wind and keep off the bacon and beans.'

The kids roared. The dads holding beer glasses roared.

And so it went on. Uncle Bernie would make embarrassing jokes at Uncle Kevin's expense, and he'd take it all in like a dustbin.

'The following magic words must be sung to the tune of the national anthem, my young apprentice, in order for the disappearing trick to work,' said Uncle Bernie, as he emptied two tins of beans, a tin of chopped tomatoes, a pint of milk, two yoghurts and a tin of Heinz spaghetti into his magician's top hat and tapped it twice with his black and white tipped magic wand.

'Owar, Tanar, Siam.'

'Oh what an arse I am,' sang Uncle Kevin as Uncle Bernie tipped the contents of the top hat on to his head, and the crowd roared.

'Not loud enough deputy,' said Uncle Bernie.

The performance of 'Morningtown Ride' Uncle Kevin gave in the heats of that year's Junior Showtime Talent Competition was one of the high

© 2006 Garry Burnett and Crown House Publishing Ltd – *Mrs Ockleton's Rainbow Kite and Other Tales: Thinking Through Literature*

points of the week. He started off quite low but then just seemed to get higher and higher. Apparently he displayed a larger vocal range than Cleo Laine and his three and a half octaves span will always be regarded by the resident band as something of a record in the history of the competition, to say nothing of the five key changes.

*Train whistle blowing makes a sleepy noise*
*Underneath the blanket go all the girls and boys*

Uncle Kevin's first car was a customised black Ford Anglia and he used to have one of those personalised name sunstrips across the top of the windscreen – you know, like some people have 'Joanne and Dave' or 'Tina and Brian' – only Uncle Kevin's said 'Me and Our Lass', which was fine until you had a lift from him and then you didn't half get some funny looks from people on the pavement. He was so well known on Newbridge Road that when he tooted his horn at pretty girls walking by they wouldn't even bother looking around before they stuck two fingers up at him.

'She fancies me really,' he said, taking Craven Street corner on two wheels.

Why Uncle Kevin used to hang about with me I'll never know, but he always seemed to have the need to put me *down*, perhaps in order to put himself *up* and, set in the context of some embarrassing showdown involving an extortionate gamble, I inevitably became the loser whatever the outcome anyway.

When I started karate lessons and he offered to give me a lift to 'see how I was doing', my heart sank. You see he'd done all that 'stuff' already, seen all the Bruce Lee films and therefore knew all of the fancy moves.

'Hold that pad up,' he said at the interval, 'And I'll show you a "snake strike".'

Sensei Sangwin asked him if he'd mind taking his shoes off when he was on the mats as Uncle Kevin limbered up to concentrate all the force his flabby arms could muster for the delivery of the killer blow. I don't know if it was the large split in the backside of his purple and brown loons which revealed his orange 'Y' fronts underneath, or the loud cooing which caused the rest of the dojo to turn around to witness, but when his 'snake strike' bent back the tips of his fingers at right angles to his palm he let out a girlish shriek like a cockatoo on fire.

'Can you get the bus home, wart,' he said, cradling his injured hand and dancing from foot to foot, 'I've got to get off.'

'Okay,' I said, relieved, as I looked down at the big toes poking through the frayed corners of his socks patterned with holly and robins and Christmas puddings.

It was the middle of June.

Uncle Kevin was stopped by the police on the way to the Hull Royal Infirmary for dangerous driving, because every time he took his good hand off the steering wheel the car veered half way across the road. He had a month off work with that sprained wrist, which meant 'close season' for the darts and snooker and, apparently, gave me an unfair advantage from now on any way, so all outstanding debts were cancelled.

We used to go together to a swimming club called The Dolphins every Monday night at East Hull baths. My mum made me go with Uncle Kevin because (can you believe it) she said he was more 'grown-up'. I can remember my first swimming instructor, Charlie Pound, who used to walk patiently beside me in the water, holding me level until I could float by myself. Isn't it funny how some memories remain so clear? I can still smell the chlorine and feel the clammy heat, still picture the wire clothes baskets and shiny number tags on elastic bands that we used to throw into the deep end to dive for. At the end of term gala I was the only one to jump in at the start of the 'beginner's' race – everyone else dived in and sped across as if they were cross-channel veterans, leaving me to doggy-paddle in last to the great guffaws of Uncle Kevin, spectating on the side.

He had entered the 'who could swim underwater the longest race' and he told me before the start that he had developed a new technique for swimming further that involved using less oxygen and that the others wouldn't have a chance now that he'd perfected it (in the bath). The only trouble was that for most of the race this meant he had to lie face down, perfectly still in the water, which, as you can imagine, soon had the crowd muttering its impatient concern.

'Is that lad alright?' said one.

© 2006 Garry Burnett and Crown House Publishing Ltd – *Mrs Ockleton's Rainbow Kite and Other Tales: Thinking Through Literature*

'Did 'e hit 'is head on the bottom when he dived in?' said another.

'Give 'im a nudge Ken, we wanna be starting the relays before ten.'

So Mr Moody the timekeeper picked up the huge shepherd's crook they used to fish the beginners out of the deep end and prodded Uncle Kevin until he got a response.

'Nobody said owt to me about a time limit,' he complained, letting out a huge belch at the baying crowd and glaring with bloodshot eyes like the victim of a wrongful arrest.

If anything, his gambling seemed to get worse as I grew older and almost everything became the subject of a bet.

There used to be this huge barrel, a big version of the kind hamsters have, in the children's play park at Hornsea Pottery and all the kids would run around in it as fast as they could until somebody tripped and everybody would fall over. There were loads of accidents as kids were trampled and flung.

Funny, but you don't see them so much nowadays.

'I'll bet you lot,' said my Uncle Kevin to us kids, 'That I can press my hands against the top and go around like a Catherine Wheel. You know, in a star shape. I'll bet you.'

''ow much?' said some snotty kids nearby.

'All the money in this pocket,' he replied, slapping his pants pocket to make it jingle. 'Oh yes,' I thought, 'I've heard that one before. He'd never put his hand in his pocket to pay a bet in his life. It'd be double or quits if he lost anyway, so I didn't hold out much hope.

'Go on then,' said the kids and they began treading the barrel to pick up speed.

'1, 2, 3 – now!' said Uncle Kevin as he locked his arms against the roof of the barrel and cartwheeled over beautifully, legs stiff, arms locked and his podgy face a bright pink. And immediately as he turned over, out rained all of the money he'd wagered.

It's a good job those kids left his car keys or we'd have been stuck. One of them just kept running inside the barrel to keep it turning with Uncle Kevin locked inside it while the other filled his pockets and legged it.

'Serves you right porky,' one of them shouted back. 'How about "double or quits"? You catch us and you can have your money back.'

But they were long gone by the time he'd recovered from his dizziness and he was left on the grass muttering something about the effects of 'G' force.

When Lance who owned the chip shop asked Uncle Kevin if he liked 'scampi' and he replied 'Oh aye, I like all the Walt Disney films', I could have curled up and died right there in front of the whole queue.

'The 'Lovebites Helpline' is probably under 'M' for medical I said to him one day as he flicked through the directory with the telephone on his lap.

'Har, har, very funny,' he said. 'Listen to James Bond. I don't exactly see 'em lining up for you.'

'That's cause he's got his eye on that lass on the checkouts at the Vivo,' said my dad. 'She goes to his school. He hasn't popped the question yet but at least we get all our shopping done fast.'

'You can get lost, you two. It's got nothing to do with you,' I hissed.

*'It's got nothing to do with you,'* mimicked Uncle Kevin, lighting a half-finished tab-end in the corner of his mouth. 'Anyway what's the matter with you? Have you gorram?'

'What?'

'Spots on your borram.'

'Careful or he'll hit you with his han'bag,' laughed my dad.

'Why must I be-ee a teenager in a love,' sang Uncle Kevin.

He was wearing torn, almost crotchless jeans, an orange vest and a baseball cap with GAP written across the forehead.

The last I'd heard of Uncle Kevin, his house had nearly been re-possessed because of gambling. His wife had made him go to all sorts of counselling group sessions but I don't think they'd worked. After his last court case he was given a grant to start his own business, so he bought an

© 2006 Garry Burnett and Crown House Publishing Ltd – *Mrs Ockleton's Rainbow Kite and Other Tales: Thinking Through Literature*

old ambulance and converted it into an ice-cream van, from which he proceeded to sell smuggled cigarettes and drink from off the docks.

Beneath 'Mr Whippy's Ice Cream' he had stencilled the words 'Mind that Chilled', but you could always tell it was his van coming anyway because when it played the jangly bell theme tune to 'Lawrence of Arabia', out of nowhere all of these fat, unshaven men with trodden down slippers would appear, like the living dead, hurrying out to stock up on their duty frees.

Never any kids, and never for ice-cream.

Typical.

## Vocabulary

| | |
|---|---|
| **Lark** | play |
| **Loons** | flared baggy trousers fashionable in the 1960s |
| **Vivo** | a local Hull supermarket chain |

# 4 Uncle Kevin
## TEACHERS' NOTES

Pupils will have opportunities to attain at the following Key Stage 3 National Curriculum levels:

### En 2 (Reading)

Pupils will have opportunities to demonstrate reading skills at the following levels:

*At level 5a*

a   To show understanding
    Develop inference
    Select appropriate evidence
b   Identify key features, themes and characters
c   Pick out supportive evidence, quotes to support a point of view
d   Understand how texts are organised (and use similar organisational strategies in own work)
e   Compare and contrast texts
f   Discuss the degree of success the author has achieved literary objectives

*At level 6a*

g   Read and discuss a wide range of texts
h   Identify *layers* of meaning
i   Identify the effects and significance of texts
j   Express a personal response to texts with reference to language, structure and themes

*At level 7a*

k   Select and synthesise information

### En3 (Writing)

Pupils will have opportunities to demonstrate writing skills at the following levels:

*At level 6a*

a   To write to engage the reader's interest
b   To use appropriate form and structure

Although Uncle Kevin is very much based on a real person and these are memories of real events shaped to form the story, I did model the character of Uncle Kevin on several prototypes, including Selwyn Froggett, Brian Potter and someone actually called Kevin. In his Introduction, Peter Thomas mentions several others who belong to the same stable: 'Like the great creations of flawed character, Pickwick, Falstaff, Del Trotter or Captain Mainwaring, (Garry's) characters too are shaped by the absurd collisions of ego and circumstance, of ambition and failure. His Uncle Kevin, in his own eyes a stylish winner in Life's lotteries is, in reality, a walking example of dire failure, but he is sustained against the pain of reality by unperishing self-esteem.' The characters Charles and Tom in the film *Four Weddings and a Funeral* have a more sophisticated knack for the embarrassing *faux pas*. Kevin's lack of *interpersonal* intelligence often manifests in relationships and situations that demand social graces.

# Understanding Uncle Kevin

In order to understand the character Uncle Kevin a little better it is worth analysing how he affects other people through what he says and does.

Read the following two extracts from Richard Curtis's *Four Weddings and a Funeral*.

## The 'David Cassidy' speech

(When Charles runs after Carrie to try to tell her he loves her.)

CHARLES Sorry. Sorry. I just … this is a really stupid question … particularly in view of our recent shopping excursion … but I just wondered if by any chance … I mean, obviously not, because I am just some git who's only slept with nine people, but I just wondered … I really feel … ahm … In the short, to recap in a slightly clearer version … in the words of David Cassidy, in fact, while he was still with the Partridge Family … 'I think I love you', and I just wondered whether by any chance you wouldn't like to … no, no of course not … I'm an idiot, he's not. Excellent. Excellent. Fantastic. Lovely to see you. Sorry to disturb … better get on.

(*He turns away*) F***

CARRIE That was very romantic …

CHARLES Well, I thought it over a lot, you know, I wanted to get it just right … Important to have said it I think.

CARRIE Said what exactly?

CHARLES Said … you know … what I just said … about … David Cassidy.

(*She moves forward*)

CARRIE You're lovely.

1 How would you describe Charles's attempt to tell Carrie he loves her? (give examples)
2 How does she react?
3 Have you or has anybody you know ever had an awkward experience trying to ask someone else out? Write out the experience in whatever form you think is most suitable (for example, play, story, factual account).

## Tom's Best Man Speech

TOM Ahm … when Bernard told me he was getting engaged to Lydia, I congratulated him because all his other girlfriends had been such complete dogs … although, may I say how delighted we are to have so many of them here this evening …

(*Gareth is loving it. He's alone.*)

TOM I'm particularly delighted to see Camilla, who many of you will probably remember as the first person Bernard asked to marry him. If I remember rightly, she told him to 'sod off' … and lucky for Lydia that she did!

1 Explain why Tom's speech causes people such embarrassment.
2 Uncle Kevin is constantly embarrassing the young boy with the things he says and does. Look back at the story 'Uncle Kevin' and find three examples of this.
3 What do you think is the boy's attitude to Uncle Kevin embarrassing him all the time?
4 Write a mock 'problem page' letter to a teenage magazine about Uncle Kevin. Compose the reply you think you might receive, giving good advice on how to cope with the situation!
5 Imagine a new TV series starring Uncle Kevin is to be made. Who would you cast in the main role and why?
6 Write a short story with the title 'It was so embarrassing' that could be about someone you know or a time when you yourself were involved in an embarrassing situation.

*Or*

7 Do you have an embarrassing relative like Uncle Kevin? Have they ever put you in situations where you almost wished you could be invisible you have been so embarrassed? Write a description of the person and the incident you were involved in.

© 2006 Garry Burnett and Crown House Publishing Ltd – *Mrs Ockleton's Rainbow Kite and Other Tales: Thinking Through Literature*

# 5 The Man in Black

© 2006 Garry Burnett and Crown House Publishing Ltd – *Mrs Ockleton's Rainbow Kite and Other Tales: Thinking Through Literature*

> It is in the night, imagining some fear
> How easy is a bush supposed a bear
>
> WILLIAM SHAKESPEARE,
> *A Midsummer Night's Dream*

I must say, when he 'babysat' for us my Uncle Kevin's bedtime stories were nothing like my Auntie Carole's which, being usually about castles and princesses and wizards, were fairly tame in comparison. For a start his stories always had a hero called Kevin in them, and when the mutant monster had been slayed in a bloodbath of carnage and mutilation and the hero had saved the kingdom, or something, Uncle Kevin would end it by saying …

'This is your storyteller, the Man in Black.'

You see he wanted us to think he was like Valentine Dyall who used to tell ghost stories on the radio in a really scary, deep silky voice. In his frayed purple jeans and 'Roadrunner' T-shirt, Uncle Kevin was far less convincing, though we still often ended up keeping the bedroom light on until my mum and dad came in for fear of attack by one of his vampire-monster creations.

'I ought to write some of these down,' he said proudly one night, when my little brother was so frightened he squashed into my bottom bunk bed with me. 'You never know, I could be the new Ronald Dahl.'

And I sometimes think there was a kind of conspiracy between my dad and him to see who could frighten us the most. On Friday nights my brother and I would be allowed to stay up late to watch the *Hammer House of Horror*, which often featured vampires, werewolves, mummies or the fiend who used to frighten me the most – Frankenstein's monster. There seemed to be loads of Frankenstein films – *The Bride of Frankenstein*, *The Curse of Frankenstein*, *Frankenstein meets Godzilla* and so on, and I wouldn't be surprised if there had been a *Frankenstein meets Uncle Kevin* made somewhere, too horrific for general release.

I don't know what it was about the Frankenstein films in particular that used to scare me so much but when this expressionless, white-faced monster came lumbering out of the fog and you could see the horrific scars all over his hands and neck, I used to get ever so frightened. In one of them he was seen holding the hand of this sweet-looking little girl with ringlets who had no idea that he had the brain of a psychopathic maniac, and a great crowd of angry, torch-bearing villagers would end up storming the castle to avenge the murder, only to have boulders or boiling oil rained down on them by the hunchback Igor, cackling madly and with his hair blowing wildly everywhere. Believe me, I've had more than one screaming nightmare about running away as he chased me while I slipped desperately on muddy ground, unable to escape.

But the worst thing about all of this was that my dad, who used to sit up to watch these films with us, used to *pretend* to fall asleep on the settee in the middle of them and then, when the music began building up to a really scary bit and you just knew something terrible was going to happen, he would suddenly sit bolt upright with a loud scream, slapping the arm of the settee as he did so.

And of course all of this made going to bed even harder because I shared a bedroom with my little brother and we had this rule that 'the last one in bed turns the light off'. It often led to fights, or one of us pushing the other one down the stairs, especially on a night after the *Hammer House of Horror* had been on, when we were even more scared at the prospect of running the six or seven feet from the light switch to the bed. One night my brother even took a sweeping brush handle to bed with him so he could poke off the switch while he was tucked under the sheets.

'What's all that carrying on?' shouted my dad up the stairs one night, after a particularly violent set-to, whereupon we were immediately tight-lipped and still.

'Zzzzzzz,' snorted my brother, unrealistically.

'Do you think I'm daft?' said my dad (we both nodded).

'If there's any more noise, I'll be up there,' he warned, closing the living room door.

'*What's all that carrying on?*' said my brother, who knew all of my dad's sayings and could do a perfect imitation of him. Sometimes he even fooled my mum when she telephoned from work by pretending to be my dad – the conversation could go on for ages before she realised.

'*Do you fink I'm daft? I'll be up there,*' he said. 'Listen, next time I'll bet he says "I'm not telling you again".'

© 2006 Garry Burnett and Crown House Publishing Ltd – *Mrs Ockleton's Rainbow Kite and Other Tales: Thinking Through Literature*

SECTION 1 | **The Man in Black**

'I'm not telling you again,' shouted my dad, muffled from the living room.

'So button it,' whispered my brother, loudly.

'So button it,' shouted my dad. 'And get to sleep.'

I couldn't help but laugh out loud as we poured scorn on the common enemy. My brother always seemed to get it just right, but especially where my dad was concerned.

'What do you think he'll say next?' I squealed, kicking my legs under the sheets in excitement.

'Well, let's see, we have a choice,' said my brother. 'We've got either "This is your last chance" or "If I've told you once, I've told you a th …"'

'Right,' said my dad who had been listening in the hallway. 'I heard that' and he began to clump up the stairs.

'You watch,' said my brother. 'I'll struggle. He can never hit the target when you struggle.'

I don't think my dad believed my brother when he said he must have been 'talking in his sleep'. He didn't half struggle when my dad tried to smack his bottom though – and he didn't half 'yelp' when he hit the mark. I always used to think at times like this that though he was so much younger than me, he wasn't frightened of anything and it made me feel ashamed that I was such a 'scaredy cat' myself.

When the lights were finally turned out and the room went dark, then the night noises began. Every creak and snap amplified ten times in the silence and I was never quite sure if those footsteps climbing the stairs were from our house or from Uncle Butch next door. Or maybe it could have been one of Uncle Kevin's monsters out looking for a bit of a human flesh and blood supper. I daren't even lift my head to look.

Sometimes on summer nights, when Billy Smart's circus pitched in East Park near to where we lived, I would lie very still as the sounds of elephants trumpeting or the roaring of tigers and lions in their cages drifted down the silent streets and into my open window. Alone listening to the sleepers in the house breathing I would squeeze my eyes tight shut in the darkness just in case a pair of spangled green eyes suddenly blinked open from the dark corners of the bedroom and a huge escaped beast behind them sat up on its haunches, preparing to spring.

In the winter time or on dark nights whenever my mum or dad asked me to run an errand to Mrs Butter's corner shop at the end of the street, although I would never admit it, it caused a great fluttering panic to seize me. Our street was lined with an avenue of tall trees whose branches caused fluttering shadows to be cast over the pavement and road, and the only illumination came from a string of weak lamps, set wide apart and on opposite sides of the street. Occasionally the windows of houses whose curtains were open cast light across the path, but never enough to make much difference to the general gloom.

Anybody who saw me step out into the street, look around to see if there were people I could walk near to, or any cars shining their headlights up or down the street, would probably think they were watching a lunatic when they saw what happened next. You see by now I was so afraid of the night that, in my mind, every darkened alcove contained some *Hammer House of Horror* devil waiting to stalk me once my back was turned. So I ended up running from street lamp to street lamp across the road and back until I reached the Southcoates Lane end of the street, twice the real distance at least because of the zig-zag route I had taken, which must give you an indication of the lengths I was prepared to go to.

And even now as I look back, I see myself sometimes in and sometimes out of darkness, appearing and disappearing in occasional pools of light.

Before it was called 'Flamingoland', Flamingo Park Zoo, as it was then known, was a very different place from what it is now – there was no funfair and the nearest they had to a 'ride' was what was laughingly called 'The Jungle Cruise'. Into the 'paddle steamer' we would all squash for a trip to 'The Kongo' and the boat, manned by two huge, fat, part-time amateur wrestlers called 'The Klondyke Brothers', would lurch across a muddy coloured lake where we would be sprayed by plastic elephants and hippos, and a motorised crocodile slid unconvincingly into the water.

At the end of the 'cruise' we were all ushered into the dark boathouse to see what we were told was the zoo's 'latest acquisition'. At the far end of the dimly lit room was a stout-barred cage in virtual darkness and one day my fearless little brother, Uncle Kevin and me squeezed through to get a better look.

'Ladies and gentlemen, don't get *toooo* close,' said our guide Jake Klondyke. 'Because in this cage is a unique and very dangerous animal. You see, what we have here is the near extinct meat-eating mountain gorilla from darkest Borneo – a very rare animal indeed. Now the reason we have kept the room in such dark conditions is because the jungle is so dense in the part of the world he comes from, that the sun never reaches the floor through the thick canopy of tropical foliage. You must not under any circumstances get too near to him ladies and gentlemen otherwise I'm afraid I cannot be held responsible for what might happen. He has the strength of ten men and we have had to build this specially fortified cage to hold him in!'

Well!

Uncle Kevin, my brother and me stood intently listening to this terrifying description when all of a sudden the silver-backed, meat-eating mountain gorilla charged out of the dark recess at the fortified door and the crowd lurched back as if it were on a sinking ship.

'RRROOOOOOAAAAAAAAARRRRRRR!!!' yelled the gorilla, as loudly as he could into his hidden microphone.

'Try not to be alarmed, ladies and gentlemen,' Jake Klondyke reassured us. 'But just remember not to get within his arm's length because the unique feature of the silver-backed mountain gorilla,' he said, seeing my wide-eyed little brother on the front row, 'is they are particularly fond of *heeeeoooman* flesh.'

And then once again the 'gorilla' attacked the cage door with all his might, 'RRROOOOOOAAAAAAAAARRRRRRR!!!!!!' he roared, as the fortified door flew open and out he swaggered into the rapidly disappearing crowd.

'Bloody 'ell,' said Uncle Kevin as he pushed past the screaming women and children charging to the exit and then he legged it, off into the distance with the hysterical crowd following.

It wasn't until I was well past the swimming pool home of 'Cuddles, the Killer Whale' that I realised my brother wasn't with me and when I saw Uncle Kevin peeping round the corner of Baboon Island *on his own* I knew he had been left at the mercy of the beast.

'Oh, err, I've had a bad stomach, I had to nip to the lav. Don't you tell your mam,' said a sweaty Uncle Kevin guiltily, before I even asked him where he'd been.

What would I tell her? I was supposed to hold my brother's hand, *all the time*. I could just imagine what she'd say:

'Where's your brother?'

'I'm sorry mam, he got eaten by this great big gorilla.'

'Why didn't you hold his hand?'

'Because I didn't want to be eaten too.'

I couldn't win, whatever the outcome.

I'd never seen anyone with their hair actually standing on end before but I was just so relieved that my brother was next to the boathouse holding 28-stone Slim Klondyke's hand I didn't even notice it at first, or the discarded gorilla suit head which was lying on the entrance floor.

'Course I knew it was a fella in a suit all the time,' said Uncle Kevin later. 'I just went along with it so you'd take it all in.'

But we were not so convinced. There was genuine terror written on that pasty speckled face as he broke the Kirby Misperton all-comers record for the 200 metres.

Strange really, because, after all, you would have thought such a unique and inspirational experience could have provided a wealth of material for a renowned storyteller like the *Man in Black*.

© 2006 Garry Burnett and Crown House Publishing Ltd – *Mrs Ockleton's Rainbow Kite and Other Tales: Thinking Through Literature*

SECTION 1    **The Man in Black**

# 5 The Man in Black
## TEACHERS' NOTES

Pupils will have opportunities to attain at the following Key Stage 3 National Curriculum levels:

### En 2 (Reading)

Pupils will have opportunities to demonstrate reading skills at the following levels:

#### At level 5a

a  To show understanding
   Develop inference
   Select appropriate evidence
b  Identify key features, themes and characters
c  Pick out supportive evidence, quotes to support a point of view
d  Understand how texts are organised (and use similar organisational strategies in own work)

#### At level 6a

h  Identify *layers* of meaning
j  Express a personal response to texts with reference to language, structure and themes

#### At level 7a

k  Select and synthesise information

### En3 (Writing)

Pupils will have opportunities to demonstrate writing skills at the following levels:

#### At level 6a

a  To write to engage the reader's interest
b  To use appropriate form and structure

#### At level 7a

c  Show clear sense of purpose and audience

This story (also included on the CD) has a strong performance element and depends for its success very much on the pace and timing of the delivery. Discussions might centre as such on aspects of performance. Activities reflect the emphasis in the story on oracy and the appropriateness of language for audience and purpose. Pupils are encouraged to exercise linguistic intelligence and to make evaluative judgements on the effectiveness of different language registers. Activities also encourage the student to focus on the skill of storytelling itself (or, in Uncle Kevin's case, the lack of it).

The opening sequence, although a composite of various incidents and events, was actually inspired by a line in a Michael Rosen poem in which he remembers mimicking his father with his brother as they lay in adjoining beds.

I'm relieved that my own dad enjoys these stories, although the 'real' Uncle Kevin has no idea yet that his fifteen minutes of fame is upon him. I would pursue one of my comic heroes Peter Kay to play Kevin should there ever be a chance this might reach the small screen.

This story can be found on Track 2 of the audio CD accompanying this book.

**The Man in Black** | SECTION 1

# The Man in Black

1 Why do you think the story is called 'The Man in Black'?

2 How does the title quote (shown below) connect with the story? Why do you think it was chosen?

> It is in the night, imagining some fear
> How easy is a bush supposed a bear
>
> WILLIAM SHAKESPEARE,
> *A Midsummer Night's Dream*

3 Read the section beginning with the following extract again:

> 'What's all that carrying on?' said my brother, who knew all of my dad's sayings and could do a perfect imitation of him. Sometimes he even fooled my mum when she telephoned from work by pretending to be my dad – the conversation could go on for ages before she realised.

How do the two brothers make fun of their father when they should be going to sleep?

4 Read the following extract again:

> I don't know what it was about the Frankenstein films in particular that used to scare me so much but when this expressionless, white-faced monster came lumbering out of the fog and you could see the horrific scars all over his hands and neck, I used to get ever so frightened. In one of them he was seen holding the hand of this sweet-looking little girl with ringlets who had no idea that he had the brain of a psychopathic maniac, and a great crowd of angry, torch-bearing villagers would end up storming the castle to avenge the murder, only to have boulders or boiling oil rained down on them by the hunchback Igor, cackling madly and with his hair blowing wildly everywhere. Believe me, I've had more than one screaming nightmare about running away as he chased me while I slipped desperately on muddy ground, unable to escape.

What is it that most frightens the boy?

Write in a similar way about something which has frightened you. Could it be something irrational and silly? Might there be a reason for the fear?

5 Which of the writer's phrases and descriptions are the most effective ones in creating humour about Uncle Kevin at 'Flamingoland'?

6 How is the story 'similar' to the prose extract 'Tell your story Thomas Leaf' (see resource sheet 'Tell your story Thomas Leaf' on page 91)?

7 Write a 'conversation' piece similar in style to the boy's account of bedtime. This might be about another home situation or may even be written as a sketch.

© 2006 Garry Burnett and Crown House Publishing Ltd – *Mrs Ockleton's Rainbow Kite and Other Tales: Thinking Through Literature*

SECTION 1 | **The Man in Black**

# 6 Egging

> Fair seed time had my soul, and I grew up
> Fostered alike by beauty and by fear
>
> WILLIAM WORDSWORTH, *The Prelude*, Book 1

What with all of the different collecting 'crazes' I went through as a child, it's a wonder I could keep a track of myself – PG Tips tea cards, football stickers, Dinky toy cars, Thunderbirds, football, conkers, 'Billy the Cat' *Dandy* comics, roller skates, Captain Scarlet figures. Oh I could go on and on. Hardly a day went by when somebody didn't bring their unwanted 'doubles' to school to swap and you would see large gatherings at playtime in the bike sheds as people traded or made up sets in the playground mini market place.

My cousin Terry and I collected birds' eggs, which we kept in old biscuit tins half-filled with sawdust, hollowing out little beds in order to tuck them carefully into neat rows of descending size or colour. We never placed the egg straight in of course – it had to be 'blown' first in order to remove the contents. This meant taking a sharp pin and ever so delicately making a little hole in the shell, perforating the skin at each end to release the albumen and allow the egg debris to salivate from the shell. Sometimes, if there were the early stages of growth, it might need a little extra encouragement in the form of a gentle blow, but we had usually detected this already, either by floating the egg in a cup of water or holding it to a bright light to 'x-ray' it for shadows.

Then, when the egg had been drained and any crusted yolk or fragments of shell swabbed and removed, it could finally take its place in the collection.

There was never any fun in swapping eggs though, which makes me think that probably the most important part of the whole exercise was the thrill of locating and securing the prize and not the static assortment of hollow coloured shells in the box.

It was around March that we began our ritualistic trawls, peering into the thickening hedgerows for tell-tale black clots in the veiny branches that gave away the locations of nests, or a dark fan of tail-feathers poking over the edge of the nest which betrayed the mother bird cosseting a clutch of eggs beneath.

We were intrepid in our pursuit of them, braving all perils of height and weather, so that for the spring months our hands were scratched raw by hawthorn spikes as a result of reaching through the many-tangled branches, our fingers full of spells from splintered barbs and sharp needles of thistles and bramble thorns. It never occurred to us that we might be doing anything wrong and when my parents tried to appeal to our consciences by saying things like 'How would you like it if somebody had come along and taken you away from your mum and dad?', it never really had any effect.

So, as the season progressed, our collections grew. Dunnock's eggs, like shiny turquoise sugar sweets, nestled next to Moorhen's, coffee coloured and speckled with maroon twists and curls, and Blackbird's (far more common and easy to find), dull sea-green with ginger freckles. We knew all the names of the birds and their eggs and eventually the shapes of their nests, because we had this battered old Observer's book to help us.

The last time I ever went egging was one cool Good Friday in April, when our Terry and me set off to walk the derelict Withernsea railway line to the water-ski pond at Keyingham. Our school satchels, packed with jam sandwiches in waxy bread bags, bits of broken chocolate Easter egg in coloured foil and plastic commando flasks filled with diluted orange squash, slapped against our shoulders in time with the crunching of cinders beneath our feet as we left the estate, the woodyards and the smoking dockside chimneys behind us.

Our eyes were wide open for give-away signs in upper branches, although we were supposedly looking for water-birds on this expedition when our Terry suddenly held up his hand and whispered 'nest!' loudly as he pointed to a thick clump of twigs level with our eyeline at the top of a steep bank. From where we stood we saw one tawny green Magpie's egg.

'We'll have that,' said our Terry.

'You'll never climb to it,' I said.

'You wanna bet?' he replied, skidding down the slope on the backside of his jeans.

'And even if you did, how would you get the egg down without breaking it?'

He had obviously decided he would sort that problem out when he came to it as he clambered

© 2006 Garry Burnett and Crown House Publishing Ltd – *Mrs Ockleton's Rainbow Kite and Other Tales: Thinking Through Literature*

quickly up the branches of the tree, many of which bent and split as he did so. Holding on precariously with one hand, he gently reached into the nest and held the egg skyward for inspection.

'I can't tell,' he said. 'It's not bright enough. Here y'are, catch.'

'No don't!' I said through the tangled mass of twigs. 'It'll hit a branch and smash.'

'But, I'll need both me hands to climb,' he said, suddenly looking very small as he swung like a trapeze artist on an upper branch. 'I know,' he said as he puffed out his cheeks like a guinea pig, 'I'll put it in me mouth.'

And he placed it on his outstretched tongue and took it in.

I'm not sure what it was that caused him to lose his grip as he began to descend, but the thick horizontal branch that stopped him as he crashed ground ward, bending him into a 'v' across his stomach, pushed the wind out of him along with the contents of his mouth.

'Whoof!' he said, as the egg sploshed on to the hard mud and broken fragments of shell splintered in the bloody glue that had spilled on the dark ground. Then, as I looked more closely I saw a tiny pink foetus with purplish sightless eyes stretch its neck in the coolness of the afternoon air.

Life …

I quickly picked up a flat piece of slate lying nearby and pressed it down hard on to the dying chick with my foot, feeling it give and spread under its weight until it finally rested flat on the ground. Behind our Terry at the top of the tree the agitated mother bird dipped and fussed around the disturbed nest as he silently climbed down to join me. Without a word we both picked up our satchels and turned to head back, a great knot of guilt and grief lodged in my throat and chest.

On top of the railway bridge at the end of Seven Alleys we parted. He set off to cross the Belly Fields to his house in Victor Street and I stood for a moment to look back at the moving dock cranes and the pointed green hanging tower of Hull Prison. And for just a moment, as I stood there and looked up at their great height and the gulls wheeling in the blowing clouds over the estuary, I would have sworn I could feel the motion of the world, rolling the horizon towards me.

Then I headed back down Southcoates Lane, past the Blue Heaven club and the tall windows of my school; past the Ravensar Arms and the closed up corner shop which belonged to old Mrs Sugden who had died.

And as I finally turned into the ten-foot for home, where small children busied with jam jars collecting caterpillars from yellow-leafed bushes, from the Sacred Heart church behind me the Easter service bells began to vault and turn, like tumblers in their tower.

## Vocabulary

| | |
|---|---|
| **Spells** | splinters |
| **Ten-foot** | a small alley, an area between houses where garages usually project into and often used by children as a play area – often not more than 'ten-foot' in width |

© 2006 Garry Burnett and Crown House Publishing Ltd – *Mrs Ockleton's Rainbow Kite and Other Tales: Thinking Through Literature*

# Egging

## TEACHERS' NOTES

Pupils will have opportunities to attain at the following Key Stage 3 National Curriculum levels:

### En1 (Speaking and Listening)

Pupils will have opportunities to demonstrate speaking and listening skills at the following levels:

*At level 5a*

c  Contribute, evaluate others' ideas, vary participation

### En 2 (Reading)

Pupils will have opportunities to demonstrate reading skills at the following levels:

*At level 5a*

a  To show understanding
   Develop inference
   Select appropriate evidence
b  Identify key features, themes and characters
e  Compare and contrast texts
f  Discuss the degree of success the author has achieved literary objectives

*At level 6a*

g  Read and discuss a wide range of texts
h  Identify *layers* of meaning

*At level 7a*

k  Select and synthesise information

### En3 (Writing)

Pupils will have opportunities to demonstrate writing skills at the following levels:

*At level 6a*

a  To write to engage the reader's interest
b  To use appropriate form and structure

*At level 7a*

c  Show clear sense of purpose and audience
e  Write confidently using a range of sentence structures

I didn't fully realise the similarities between this and Wordsworth's 'The Prelude' until my friend Peter Thomas pointed it out to me and now I begin to wonder if the theme and narrative, even though I thought they were entirely personal and rooted in autobiographical facts, were in fact somehow sub-consciously plagiarised. I hope that the exercise, comparing Wordsworth's immortal description of the 'nesting' episode in 'The Prelude' in some way illustrates what I mean.

At the point I was at in my writing career I felt I had to do something which was both moving, serious and utterly devoid of the trivial and ironic humour that characterises many of the other stories, especially those featuring Uncle Kevin. He was at one stage featured in an early draft of this story, but was removed because his appearance detracted from the overall tone I wanted to create.

The poem 'A dead sparrow' by Brian Gile has haunted and intrigued me since I was fourteen and is taken from the celebrated *Viewpoint* anthology. I am particularly curious about the last line 'Man, Jack, they clap …', which I am still not fully sure I understand – though it has for me a kind of dismissive rhythmical charm that is a perfect balance to the sonorous tone of the first half. I wanted in my own story to have an obvious association with Easter, eggs as vessels of new life and resurrection.

The autobiographical subject matter is nothing to be proud of though I'm sure that in discussions with children about the many cruelties they have perpetrated in their own childhoods, horrors equal to this are certain to be revealed.

For further activities related to coming to terms with death see the activities connected with 'Mrs Ockleton's Rainbow Kite' on pages 107–8.

SECTION 1 | **Egging**

# Egging

1. How do the boy's parents try to persuade him to stop collecting birds' eggs?
2. What evidence is there in the story that the boy is an 'expert' on the subject of birds and their eggs?
3. Why, do you think, did the boy decide to kill the chick?
4. How did this affect the boy and how did his attitude change?
5. The story ends on the simile 'like tumblers in their tower'. What is the author trying to describe?
6. Why do you think this is an effective way of ending the story?

Now read the following extract 'Nesting' from an autobiographical poem 'The Prelude' Book 1 by the poet William Wordsworth.

Think about how this piece of writing could have influenced the writing of 'Egging'.

## Nesting

Fair seed-time had my soul, and I grew up
**Fostered** alike by beauty and by fear
Much favoured in my birth-place, and no less
In that beloved Vale to which **erelong**
We were transplanted – there were we let loose
For sports at wider range. Ere I had told
Ten birth days, when among the mountain slopes
Frost, and the breath of frosty wind, had snapped
The last autumnal crocus, 'twas my joy
With store of **springes** o'er my shoulder hung
To range the open heights where **woodcocks** run
Along the smooth green turf. Through half the night,
**Scudding** away from snare to snare, I plied
That anxious visitation; moon and stars
Were shining o'er my head. I was alone,
And seemed to be a trouble to the peace
That dwelt among them. Sometimes it befell
In these night wanderings, that a strong desire
**O'erpowered** my better reason, and the bird
Which was the captive of another's toil
Became my prey; and when the deed was done
I heard among the solitary hills
Low breathings coming after me, and sounds
Of indistinguishable motion, steps
Almost as silent as the turf they trod.

Nor less, when Spring had warmed the cultured Vale,
Moved we as **plunderers** where the mother-bird
Had in high places built her lodge; though mean
Our object and inglorious, yet the end

Was not **ignoble**. Oh! when I have hung
Above the raven's nest, by knots of grass
And half-inch **fissures** in the slippery rock
But ill-sustained, and almost (so it seemed)
Suspended by the blast that blew **amain**
Shouldering the naked crag, oh, at that time
With what strange utterance did the loud dry wind
Blow through my ear! The sky seemed not a sky
Of earth – and with what motion moved the clouds!

WILLIAM WORDSWORTH

In each piece of writing ('Egging' and 'The Prelude' extract) how does the experience with Nature affect the boys as they are 'growing up'?

### Vocabulary

| | |
|---|---|
| **Amain** | around, about |
| **Erelong** | before long |
| **Fissures** | a narrow opening, crack |
| **Fostered** | cared for, brought up, nurtured |
| **Ignoble** | something to be ashamed of, shameful |
| **O'erpowered** | overcome, beaten |
| **Plunderers** | robbers, people who are there to take the eggs |
| **Scudding** | move quickly, skim along |
| **Springes** | snares |
| **Woodcock** | a small moorland bird |

# A dead sparrow

The poem 'A dead sparrow' by Brian Gile was a significant influence on the story 'Egging'.

## A dead sparrow

Strange how this trivial business touched
    More than you'd guess,
Seeing I'd known a viler thing.
It was in winter, when the gales
Blundered and bullied through the town:
We'd brought him in from the garden, smutched
With dirt, dragging a broken wing,
Thinking he'd mend without much fuss.
The best laid plan, you'll say, most often fails …
Of course. He died before the gales died down.

His death was a small thing, you'll say:
    Yet when I held
Jack Sparrow lifeless in my hand.
I thought I could have spelled
For you death's final murdering word.
It was so small a death: he lay
So lightly there on my palm,
It seemed, simply that death, so calm,
So small, lay there as lightly as the bird:
It seemed an easy thing to understand.

Well, since the ground was frozen fast,
    He fed the fire.
Dead bones and feathers, flesh and blood:
These give you images to last
A lifetime or a poem out,
And say nothing when all's been said.
Today, the spring flickers about
The hedge, flame-green, owl-white, heart-red;
The Easter bells turn cartwheels in their spire:
Man, Jack, they clap; wrong, right; quick, dead, quick, dead.

*Brian Gile*

**1** What was it about this 'trivial business' that 'touched' the poet?
**2** Highlight the descriptive words in the poem. What does the poet mean when he says 'These give you images to last'?
**3** Read the ends of the story and the poem once again. How could the poem have been an inspiration for 'Egging'?

## ✎ Write

Write a poem or story about a personal experience involving coming to terms with death. This could be about the first time you experienced the death of someone you were close to or it could be about the loss of a family pet or an encounter with death similar to the ones in the story and poems.

# The short story

Most good short stories are written by using certain key features. They usually include:

1 An opening – setting the scene quickly; the main character who we care about
2 A problem or a conflict or a challenge
3 A turning point or climax
4 An ending – a problem is resolved or there is a cliffhanger or a twist.

Can you find any of these features in the short story 'Egging'?

# Pair activity

Read the *opening* paragraph of 'Egging'. Working in pairs, take just one paragraph and see what you can find out about the author's style. Use the questions below to help you.

1 Who is telling this story (narrator)?
2 What tense is the narrator using and why?
3 Who is the story about and which word tells you this?
4 What stage of life is this main character at?
5 What words give a sense that this story is set in England?
6 How do these details get the reader interested? What is the author really making us do?
7 What hobbies are you and your friends into that would sum up your school years?

# Genre: types of story

What genre (type of story) do you think this might be? Circle it and explain why you have made this choice.

| Supernatural | Romance | Comedy | Biography | Horror |
| --- | --- | --- | --- | --- |
| Thriller | Autobiography | Science Fiction | Historical | |

# Individual activity: what happens next?

Read the story 'Egging' up to the word, 'Life …'.
Now you are the author, finish the end of the story as you think it should be.
Now read the real ending.

- Are you surprised at the author's ending?
- Describe how you think the narrator changes as he walks home.
- What effect do the boys' actions have on him?

© 2006 Garry Burnett and Crown House Publishing Ltd – *Mrs Ockleton's Rainbow Kite and Other Tales: Thinking Through Literature*

# Foreshadowing

This is when the author plants little hidden clues throughout the story that reveal that something serious or important is going to happen. Have you noticed the foreshadowing of the boy's cruel, unthinking act?

1. What clues does the author give us that perhaps this hobby is not perfectly innocent?
2. Why are the hunts for eggs described as 'ritualistic trawls'?
3. 'We were intrepid in our pursuit of them, braving all perils.' What attitude do the boys have towards hunting eggs?
4. The boys could spot birds by their feathers. Why does the author use the word 'betrayed'?
5. For what reason do the boys have to climb so high and through such spiky thorns to get to the nests?
6. The boys are absorbed in their own world and their hands are 'scratched raw'. What atmosphere is being set up here?
7. 'The last time I ever went egging.' How does this line change the tone of the story?

# Setting: using the senses

1. Which words highlight the physical danger of searching for eggs and did the boys enjoy this part of it?
2. What words tell us that this may be a type of 'journey' or challenge for the boys?

The author describes the natural environment very vividly. This gives us a sense of the outdoors, connecting with nature and the innocence of the boys playing, experimenting, messing about and getting dirty! In fact, we often remember childhood through colours, smells, sounds or just a feeling.

### Individual activity

Describe in writing a childhood memory by focusing on the senses. For example, fighting with friends, running away from someone, falling off your bike. It might even be a fleeting moment but concentrate on the physical sensations you experienced.

© 2006 Garry Burnett and Crown House Publishing Ltd – *Mrs Ockleton's Rainbow Kite and Other Tales: Thinking Through Literature*

SECTION 1 | **Egging**

# A language of rhythm: rhyme roulette

The author has used language in such a way as to create a special rhythm. When we read these sentences, we are naturally drawn to the flow of the words and the way they bounce off the tongue. The effect of this is to emphasise certain feelings and ideas in the words or to heighten an atmospheric setting.

## Small group activity

In a small group, allocate a reader from the group to read aloud paragraphs 5–8 to the group. Just listen to the sounds and try to identify as many types of rhyme as you can in each of the chosen paragraphs. Underline in the same colour each part of a word that has the *same sound repeated* in another word close by. Use different colours for different sounds.

This game card below will help you.

| Technique | Repeated sound (rhyme) | Example | Number of examples in passages |
|---|---|---|---|
| Alliteration | Starting consonant sounds | Terrible twosome | |
| Consonance | Middle consonant sounds | The fat kitten patters; Lost and alone | |
| Assonance | Vowel sounds | Pray, take her away; Child of silence | |
| Sibilance | s, z, sh, x sounds | Sassy Suzie shakes | |

Some lines may have more than one type of rhyme.

**Paragraph 5**
- 'tell-tale black clots'
- 'cosseting a clutch'

**Paragraph 6**
- 'scratched raw by hawthorn spikes'
- 'fingers full of spells from splintered barbs and sharp needles of thistles and bramble thorns'

**Paragraph 7**
- 'shiny turquoise sugary sweets, nestled next to Moorhen's'

**Paragraph 8**
- 'cool Good Friday'
- 'school satchels, packed with jam sandwiches in waxy bread bags, bit of broken chocolate Easter egg in coloured foil and plastic command flasks filled with diluted orange squash slapped against our shoulders'

© 2006 Garry Burnett and Crown House Publishing Ltd – *Mrs Ockleton's Rainbow Kite and Other Tales: Thinking Through Literature*

# Reading skill: inferring

1. How are the boys feeling when they find the nest? What tells us this?
2. 'You'll never climb to it.' What does this make the reader think about what could go wrong?
3. Why is it so unexpected to discover what the boy does to the chick? What is the mood of story up until this point?
4. The author points out certain buildings and places to notice when the boys are walking back. Make a list of them.
5. After all the excited chatter, why is there no dialogue with Terry on the walk home?
6. The narrator describes standing and looking up at Hull Prison with the 'gulls wheeling in the blowing clouds'. What is significant about this building for the boy and what do these circling birds make you think of?
7. The narrator describes walking 'past the Blue Heaven club … past the Ravensar Arms and the closed corner shop which belonged to old Mrs Sugden who had died.' What do the names of these places make you think of and why has the author pointed out that the shop is closed and the shop-owner is dead?
8. Why do you think the story ends with the boy listening to the Easter bells of Sacred Heart church? What do you think the boy has learned?
9. What are the children doing at the end of the story as our narrator walks past? Why has the author included this?
10. After the chick has been killed, how many words and images can you find which might be about religion or death? Explain why the author uses this imagery.

# The turning point: a moral dilemma

## ❔ Group discussion

Do you think the boy is still innocent about his actions? Do you think he went egging the next year? Think of a time when you felt tremendous guilt over something small when you were young. In what way did this change you or force you to grow up?

## ✏ Written response

Look closely at the language used in paragraphs 2–4.

1. What tells us that the boys took special care when preparing the eggs?
2. What does the author want to suggest by using 'of course', when describing how the eggs are kept?
3. The narrator carries out the preparation of the egg 'ever so delicately'. What does this tell us about the boy's character and about the activity?
4. The author describes 'hollowing out little beds'. What information does this give about the character and how he thinks of the eggs?
5. How does the author compare the process to a scientific or medical experiment? What special words are used?
6. What tells us that the boys have done this many times before?
7. The author says that there 'was never any fun in swapping eggs though'. Use your own words to describe why he feels this way.
8. Which words in this paragraph show us that the author is now an adult reflecting back on his boyhood feelings?

© 2006 Garry Burnett and Crown House Publishing Ltd – *Mrs Ockleton's Rainbow Kite and Other Tales: Thinking Through Literature*

SECTION 1 | **Egging**

# Newspaper article: types of reporting

Read the following article written by the columnist W.F. Deedes from the *Daily Telegraph* (June 10th 2004).

## Country Diary

A man appeared in court the other day, charged with taking the eggs of rare wild birds and was warned that he might go to prison for it.

What folly, I thought, and then turned my mind back to the days of my boyhood when I was addicted to raiding bird's nests and kept my spoils in the drawers of a small cabinet. There were, let me add, plenty of these little cabinets on sale. So I was not a solitary miscreant.

But what was the attraction of searching for a bird's nest, taking an egg or two and keeping a collection? Today I suppose, the motive would be mainly commercial. The egg of a very rare and protected bird is marketable. Between the ages of 8 and 12, when my Easter holidays were given over to this strange hobby, I can declare at least that my motives were not commercial, I never sold an egg in my life – nor found an egg worth selling.

My parents indulged my pursuit, usually in company with a chum from a neighbouring farm, reckoning, I suppose that it provided fresh air and healthy exercise and kept me out of more damaging mischief, but my mother laid down the rules. No more than one egg should be taken from a nest, otherwise it might be deserted. If the bird was sitting, it was not to be disturbed. I was not to climb trees above a certain height.

We lived near heavily wooded areas in those days in which birds abounded. So there were rewarding takings. Eggs of our more common birds have beautiful colouring. Jackdaws are not pretty birds, but their speckled eggs have a great charm. The two white eggs laid by the wood pigeon are dull, but pigeons build high, so under mother's rules were out of bounds.

The delicate art was blowing a captured egg. This called for a very small hole at one end of the egg and a slightly larger hole at the other end. Then, with lips to the smaller hole, you blew the contents, leaving an empty shell for the drawer in the cabinet.

There were always eggs beyond reach, just as one finds with life itself. I dreamed of finding a kestrel hawk, kingfisher or plover. All three eluded me. But just before I gave up bird's nesting, I procured the egg of a mistle thrush – such exciting colouring.

These days I walk through the woods at this season watching the birds in nesting mode, but feeling no guilt for stealing their eggs all those years ago. It was after all a relatively harmless indulgence. Neither I nor my chum endangered any species of rare bird and I learned a lot about the countryside and its ways.

Put to it, I could still dam a stream, a task my friend and I practised when bored with the search for nests. The secret of that was making a sufficient stockpile of the material you need before tackling the stream. And why did that prove of value in later life?

I learned that both in peace and war it is wise before starting any undertaking to make sure you have the material required to do the job close at hand. Bird's nesting? It was a part of growing up. I feel sad for boys denied the harmless thrill of it.

W.F. Deedes

1 What is the name of this column? What type of writing can you expect from this writer then?
2 What similarities are there between the way each author talks about the pursuit of egging?
3 He writes, 'my motives were not commercial. I never sold an egg in my life – or found one worth selling'. Are there any similarities between this feeling and the boy's feelings about why he collects eggs in Burnett's story?
4 Why did the writer's mother lay down rules? How is this similar to the boy's experience in 'Egging' by Garry Burnett?
5 Does W.F. Deedes think it was an innocent activity?
6 Does he think the man who appeared in court should go to prison?

(continued)

# Newspaper article: types of reporting (contd.)

### ✎ Write

*First …*

Write a short factual newspaper report about a man arrested for stealing rare birds' eggs.

You must create a list of facts before you write the report including:

| **What?** | **Where?** | **When?** | **How?** | **Why?** |

*Then …*

Write a different type of newspaper article. This one should not just be factual but also describe what the different opinions might be on this subject.

Which type of newspapers would you find such articles in?

# Pupil research project

Look up the story 'Spit Nolan' by Bill Naughton (1992, Creative Education, Incorporated).

What similarities are there between the way the boys describe making a kart and the process of preparing eggs in 'Egging'?

What specific 'kart-racing' terminology is used in this story?

'Spit Nolan' talks of using a 'knob of margarine' for the brakes. What kind of experiment or instruction does this sound like?

© 2006 Garry Burnett and Crown House Publishing Ltd – *Mrs Ockleton's Rainbow Kite and Other Tales: Thinking Through Literature*

SECTION 1 | **Egging**

# 7 The Mariner's Tale

© 2006 Garry Burnett and Crown House Publishing Ltd – *Mrs Ockleton's Rainbow Kite and Other Tales: Thinking Through Literature*

> So deep is the night…
>
> FRÉDÉRIC CHOPIN

'Push your hair back,' said my nana. 'Right off your face. There, now, you look just like him. That's just how your Grandad George used to have his hair styled, all slicked and neatly combed. Girls used to think he looked like a film star he was so handsome, and well-dressed. And he had the most immaculate clean finger nails. He always said that the first thing anybody noticed when you lifted a drink or shook hands was the state of your nails. And his were always scrubbed clean and filed down. Not in an 'feminate way though. Just well-groomed and cared for, as if he took a pride.

'I never knew your Grandad George to be frightened of anybody or anything – though he always blamed the priest who taught him to box for his fear of the dark. He used to send the new boys into catacombs under St Charles' where they trained, make 'em sprint past open caskets of bones and skulls. On their own too. He said it would toughen them up, make them fearless. At least so he said. All it did was give them nightmares as far as I can see. Your grandfather never forgot it. He hated the dark all his life.

'I was fifteen when I first met him and when he finally asked me out I tried not to show it, you know, to keep him on his toes, but I was thrilled, and all the other Catholic girls were jealous. He was the only boy in a family of six so his mother, as you can imagine, she worshipped him. She was called Mary too, a Conboy, Irish, from Kerry. "Just think, if you get married, there'll be two Mary Moss's in one family," she said on the first night he took me home to meet her.

'Your grandad smiled, but he never said anything. She always made me feel welcome and treated me like a daughter. The old man liked his drink and he sometimes got a bit handy. George tried to protect her, even as a bain, then when he began boxing the old man thought twice. Bloody coward he was. They say she miscarried because of him.

'Your grandad joined the Royal Navy when he was sixteen and it wasn't long before he was assigned to a boat. When he was home on leave people used to come up to us when we were out and touch his white collar for luck. He did look smart.

'He used to write as well, like you, poems and stories and songs. He sent some of them to a comedian called Izzy Vaughn who used them in his stage act. I don't think he ever paid your grandad for them though. And sometimes he wrote me poems and letters with messages that only we understood – little romantic poems and lines. I don't have a one of them now.

'We got married six months before your auntie was born.

'"Look at little Hilary, sitting in the scullery, eating up the celery," he would sing to her.

'He always used to make me laugh because he'd never wear shoes or socks if he could avoid it. He said it reminded him of being on board the ship.

'Sometimes he played the harmonica and danced at the same time – proper Irish dancing, you know with stiff arms and upper body. "Typical Irish," he would say. "The top half doesn't know what the bottom half's doing." He was so full of life. And yet he would always look out for anybody he thought was having a hard time.

'Once when he was home on leave we were on our way to a dance at the Co-op Hall when he saw two men giving this policeman a good hiding. And I mean a good hiding. Taking running kicks they were, at his face and stomach. Anyway your grandad stepped forward to help but this third fella put his arm across his chest.

'"Why?" said your granddad. "They'll kill him."

'"Silver Hatchets," said the man.

'Everybody in East Hull had heard of the Silver Hatchets gang. They ran the docks, you see. They were racketeers. Hoodlums. And you were meant to pay so much of your wages to them if you wanted to work – "taxes" they called them. Once this young lad refused to pay so they took him off and cut all the fingers off his right hand. He had a young family too. They all had two crossed axes tattooed on their right arms. Bastards they were.

'Anyway your grandad took off his jacket and shoes, pushed this man aside, and went in. I was frightened, but he went in and saved that policeman's life, he did, and took both of them out.

'The police said they were really grateful of course and your grandad was given a few shillings

© 2006 Garry Burnett and Crown House Publishing Ltd – *Mrs Ockleton's Rainbow Kite and Other Tales: Thinking Through Literature*

reward but by now word was out and he had become a marked man. He couldn't drink in the Elephant and Castle anymore without somebody watching ready to follow him if he left on his own. And before he went back to sea he never went out anywhere without Sammy Flynn or his brother Johnny with him. Sometimes I'd go to close the front curtains and see a couple of fellas under the lamp opposite look up. Your grandad said not to worry, he'd take care of it. He knew all sorts of people through boxing. But I never felt easy. They were just waiting for a chance to settle the score.

'As if we didn't have enough to think about with the "Nazzy's".

'Then I found out I was expecting your mother, so the police bought him out so he could be home with me. But he was restless. It was the thirties, he couldn't find work and it was less than a year before he joined the Merchant Navy. All the time he still trained hard and boxed, for money now. Him and Sammy Flynn. Sammy was light-heavyweight and boxed under his nickname, Porky Flynn. And your grandad went under the name of "Danny" Moss. Don't ask me why – it was something to do with his being "a registered amateur" he said. They'd go all over the place and sometimes your grandad would prize-fight to make up his money, you know, "three-rounders" or "last one standing" against the "pugs" at Hull Fair. He would take off his shirt and get in the ring with these great bruisers twice his size. I couldn't watch so our Ada would sometimes sit next to me and give a commentary.

'"It's alright, you can look now," she'd say and I never knew if I'd see him half-dead and cut to pieces, but he was always standing. And by God did we need the money.

'Father O'Kelly said he was a real "prospect". He'd won the combined forces championship and had this belt with China Fleet Championship Winner on it. He sometimes gave demonstrations at Madeley Street Baths and people bought tickets to see him. By hell he could box. By hell. If there hadn't been a war who knows.

'But in 1939 the ship he was on was taking a load of iron to Narvik in Norway when it was captured by the Germans. Your grandad and the crew were all detained in prisoner of war camps.

'Because he'd resisted they smashed his hands with rifle butts. Then one night he ran the blockade and took twelve others with him before the Germans even realised they'd escaped.

'They got away across the mountains to Sweden near Bollnas. And that's where he stayed and worked, building roads and labouring for two years before the Royal Marines "rescued" them.

'"Rescued" them … and brought him back again to this. The city was in ruins, there were bombed buildings everywhere and most of his friends were either dead or conscripted.

'He never talked much about being away when he came back – October it was. And we'd had no warning he was coming home. I thought he was dead. His mother thought he was dead. He just turned up, looking thin and pale and ill.

'And his hands. His hands were still all twisted and scarred from the beating, and he couldn't make a proper fist any more.'

Her dark eyes glittered in the fading evening light. Outside in the smoky dusk the first fireworks begin to crack and hiss. All around this city, Guy Fawkes bonfires will soon be ablaze.

'One night they were bombing the docks – all the sirens were going and he just stood on that front step while everybody ran in for the shelters. There were fires all down Belmont Street and Newbridge Road and he just stood there in his bare feet like he was on the deck of a ship.

'"Why don't they fight?" he shouted. "Why don't they fight?"

'We didn't know he was still alive. There'd been no word. And the bains didn't know him and were scared of him because there'd just been no news. Then one night I went into the front room to tell him some news and he'd gone. Our Ada said she saw him standing alone with his kit bag under Craven Street bridge, he'd joined another ship and I thought then he must have known. I was pregnant to him again, with your Auntie Jacqueline you see.

'I knew him. He couldn't just sit around and do nothing. He had to fight, any way he could.

'They say the last ship he went on was fated from the off. But then sailors are of'en superstitious, you know. His was a part of a convoy

© 2006 Garry Burnett and Crown House Publishing Ltd – *Mrs Ockleton's Rainbow Kite and Other Tales: Thinking Through Literature*

out in the Atlantic torpedoed by U-boats. They used to pick them off like sharks, circle them, sink the rescue ships, fire on the life-rafts. It all happened in the middle of the night, in the dark.

'They killed my husband,' she said, wiping her face with her sleeve. 'Twice. Twice we went through that. And I knew straight away the day that he'd died. It was the end of January, less than three weeks after he'd left and the strangest thing happened, a little bird flew in through the scullery and landed on his photograph. It just stayed for a few seconds and then flew out and off.

'I had a telegram the next day.

'The worst thing was, I never had time to properly tell him all that had happened. Or him me.

'Then afterwards his mother had a card from Sweden saying he was the father of a little boy. They think I don't know, but I bear no ill. Some young girl he'd met. There was a war on and we could all 'ave been dead for all he knew. And that boy, his son, he grew up never seeing his father's face.

'You won't write about this will you?

'You know sometimes, I sense him near. It's like … it's like I think I can smell the sea. Or I glance at you, then I have to look again because … it's like him looking back at me.

'He was awarded medals for bravery in Norway, posthumously, and I had all sorts of trophies for boxing I wanted you to have, but his father pawned them. Pawned them and pissed the money up a wall. Then there was the fire and all of his certificates and news clippings and letters and writing were lost.

'So there's nothing left of him now … but this tale.

'I don't think he'd know this city now. All the big ships have gone.

'See all the proud men lining up on Monday mornings for giro money. They used to say there was a life's work here for a skilled hand. And now … he wouldn't know this place … now.'

Beyond the darkened street, away past the threshold where my grandfather stood and over to the docks, twinkling rockets whoosh and pop like gunshots and doodle-bug sirens; running footsteps thump down ten-foots as penny bangers and jumping jacks lift dustbin lids. A frightened dog's tinny bark echoes down back alleys off Belmont Street.

Sounds of war.

'But you were his first grandson,' she continued. 'And you … are the most like him. You have his eyes, his smile, his teeth … You have his hands.'

## Vocabulary

**Bain** young child

**Ten-foot** a small alley, an area between houses where garages usually project into and often used by children as a play area – often not more than 'ten-foot' in width

© 2006 Garry Burnett and Crown House Publishing Ltd – *Mrs Ockleton's Rainbow Kite and Other Tales: Thinking Through Literature*

SECTION 1 | **The Mariner's Tale**

# 7 The Mariner's Tale

## TEACHERS' NOTES

Pupils will have opportunities to attain at the following Key Stage 3 National Curriculum levels:

### En 2 (Reading)

Pupils will have opportunities to demonstrate reading skills at the following levels:

*At level 5a*

e   Compare and contrast texts
f   Discuss the degree of success the author has achieved literary objectives

*At level 6a*

g   Read and discuss a wide range of texts

*At level 7a*

k   Select and synthesise information

The first-person monologue 'talking heads' diary places very different linguistic demands on the writer. Writing in the style of the 'talking head', sounding as 'natural' as possible whilst in-role and yet still telling a coherent tale is quite challenging. I didn't want to simply 'transcribe' the many conversations I had with my gran and I suppose one of the most important things I hoped to communicate was a sense of family continuity. The 'hands' motif was particularly important to me in doing so (hands that pray, hands that fight, hands that caress, hands that create, and so on) and with it the reminder that there is physical continuity through generations by semblance and sometimes by nature. Just before she died my gran said that she had seen my grandfather standing at the end of her bed, as he used to be. 'He's come for me,' she said. We have since made contact with the extended family in Sweden and have shared many happy times and memories together.

Thomas Hardy's 'The Whitewashed Wall' is one of those poems that, typically for Hardy, has a quiet undercurrent of poignant irony. Rather like the ending of Seamus Heaney's 'Mid Term Break', 'a four foot box, a foot for every year', the line 'under his sheet of white' says everything by saying virtually nothing and the reader is left to engage in an exercise in 'meaning' construction. I wanted my own line ('You won't write about this will you?') to carry some of that emotional impact.

Everything she said and a lot more, sadly, is true.

# Talking Heads

## Extract from 'Waiting for the Telegram' (*Talking Heads 2*)

Verity fetches a young lad in this morning. She says to him, 'You're privileged. Violet is our oldest resident.' She says, 'Spencer's going to ask you one or two questions for his school project. It's about the past.'

Poor looking lad, bonny face. Floppy clothes, shirt-tails out. I said, 'Is that your big brother's jumper?' he says, 'No. It's dead smart is this.' Gets out his exercise book, and says, 'What was it like then?' 'Well …' he said, 'Were things better or worse?'

I said, 'Well, my legs were better.'

He said he didn't mean that.

Verity comes back and he says, 'She doesn't seem to know what I'm talking about.' Verity says, 'Well, she's had a stroke. Come on, I'll find you another one.'

(*Violet is a bit upset*)

I said to Francis, 'He'd mean trams and whatnot. Strikes. Tin-baths. The war. Francis says, 'Which war?' I said, 'The proper war when all the young lads got killed.'

ALAN BENNETT

1. How is the style of 'The Mariner's Tale' modelled on that of Alan Bennett's 'talking head'?

2. What do you think are the advantages and disadvantages for the writer of using the 'talking heads' format?

# The Whitewashed Wall (1)

1 Your teacher will give you a copy of the poem 'The Whitewashed Wall' by Thomas Hardy that has been cut into strips.
2 Working in pairs, attempt to re-assemble the poem in an order that makes sense.
3 Discuss reasons why the selected order has been made. What decisions were made in the process?
4 Now look at a copy of the poem in the real order and consider the differences between the assembled version and the printed version. What decisions were made and why?

## Discussion/reflection

1 What were the clues you were looking for in order to make sense of the poem?
2 What kind of questions were you asking in order to complete the task?
3 How was your completed poem different from the actual poem written by Hardy?
4 What were you doing in order to analyse the poem (what connections, links, ideas were you trying to understand)?
5 Did you find this a useful way of learning how to understand a poem?

## Write

1 Tell the *story* of the poem in your own words.
2 Use the blank storyboard sheet 'The Whitewashed Wall (3)' to create a 'film sequence' for this poem. Base this on your story version of the poem, but use actual quotes to accompany the image for each section.
3 Who do you think the 'she' in the poem is? What makes you think this?
4 Why do you think she 'kisses to the chimney wall'?
5 Why did the 'whitener' come to paint the wall?
6 How does both the poem and story 'The Mariner's Tale' express feelings of 'loss'? Which words and phrases express this most effectively?

7 What language *patterns* can you see in the poem?
8 'Irony' means 'having more than one possible meaning'. What irony do you see in the last stanza of the poem?
9 What do you think are the main connections between 'The Whitewashed Wall' and 'The Mariner's Tale'?
10 'You have his hands.' What do you think is the importance of 'hands' in the 'The Mariner's Tale' story?

## Annotate/Create

1 Imagine that you are to be the producer of a new TV series of *Talking Heads*. 'The Mariner's Tale' has been selected to be a new episode.

   Write a letter to the actress chosen to play the grandma, giving her advice on how to prepare for the role.

   In this letter tell her 'Danny's story', how you want her to read specific parts, when to pause, when to change speed, what the mood is and so on.

2 Write your own 'talking head', using either yourself as the main speaker or someone else you know. Decide what the story will be (for example, a family memory or incident) and *how* the speaker will tell it.

© 2006 Garry Burnett and Crown House Publishing Ltd – *Mrs Ockleton's Rainbow Kite and Other Tales: Thinking Through Literature*

**The Mariner's Tale** | SECTION 1

# The Whitewashed Wall (2)

## The Whitewashed Wall

Why does she turn in that shy soft way
    Whenever she stirs the fire,
And kiss to the chimney-corner wall
    As if entranced to admire

Its whitewashed bareness more than the sight
    Of a rose in richest green?
I have known her long, but this raptured rite
    I never before have seen.

– Well, once when her son cast his shadow there,
    A friend took a pencil and drew him
Upon that flamelit wall. And the lines
    Had a lifelike semblance to him.

And there long stayed his familiar look;
    But one day, ere she knew,
The whitener came to cleanse the nook,
    And covered the face from view.

'Yes,' he said: 'My brush goes on with a rush,
    And the draft is buried under;
When you have to whiten old cots and brighten,
    What else can you do, I wonder?'

But she knows he's there. And when she yearns
    For him, deep in the labouring night,
She sees him as close at hand, and turns
    To him, under his sheet of white.

                    Thomas Hardy

# The Whitewashed Wall (3)

| Image | Words |
|-------|-------|
|       |       |
|       |       |
|       |       |
|       |       |
|       |       |
|       |       |
|       |       |

© 2006 Garry Burnett and Crown House Publishing Ltd – *Mrs Ockleton's Rainbow Kite and Other Tales: Thinking Through Literature*

**The Mariner's Tale** | SECTION 1

# 8  Twenty-six Baboons

SECTION 1 | **Twenty-six Baboons**

> The wedding guest sate on a stone
> He cannot chuse but hear
> And thus spake on that ancyent man
> The bright eyed Marinere
>
> SAMUEL COLERIDGE,
> *The Ryme of the Ancient Marinere*

'Howdy pardner,' drawled Lance as I joined the end of the queue in Barratt's fish and chip shop on Alexandra Road.

'You look like you're going to a wedding,' he added in his normal voice, eyeing up my jacket and tie before he yelled, 'G'bye now and thank ya' to another customer as she opened the door to leave.

During the week Lance ran two fish and chip shops, one on Subway Street and this one, but on weekends he was a confederate general in the West Hull American Civil War Society and dressed up in full military regalia to re-enact the great battles of the southern states. How his wife Grace put up with it I'll never know but regulars enjoyed his fry-up enough to tolerate the cat-calls and the cheeky mock 'yankee' accent with which he terrorised the more bashful.

'Waiting for fries,' he said, giving his crackling pan a great heave.

'So you're back from your holiyerderrs then Tom,' said the old woman at the front to the very damp and bedraggled looking man who had just joined the queue behind me.

'Howdy pardner,' added Lance, dipping another fresh cod into his trough of batter.

'Evening,' he nodded. 'Oh 'ello Olive, I didn't see you there, love. Yes we got back on Thursdee and by 'ell I'm frozen. You don't half feel it when you been out in the Sherringetty.'

As he spoke he mashed his bottom lip to within wiping distance of the tip of his veiny nose and as Olive craned her head around to listen I could sense that the rest of the chip shop queue, bored with the wait for chips, had also tuned into this unexpected entertainment.

'But you don't look very brown,' said Olive. 'Did you have a nice time?'

'Well,' said Tom, gurning with his lower lip, 'I'll tell yer. We were out there on shafari, but it were a queer do,' he said shaking his head. 'A queer do.'

And he suddenly began to relive some of the 'queer do' drama especially for us, mashing his rubbery red lips and frowning for effect.

'We drove through the jungle on the first day for miles and miles. There was animals everywhere – lions, shnakes, hittopotamuses. And then all of a sudden we hit this boulder in the middle of the track.'

'Well, 'ell,' said Olive. 'So what did you do?'

'Well o' course we was shtranded. But we had shtrict instructions, should an emergency situation arise to just stay inside the cab and pip the horn for the park ranger. All of a sudden, out of nowhere, came twenty-six baboons, running like hell towards us out of the bushes. They just jumped up on the bonnet and began pulling bits off.'

'Give over,' said Olive. 'So what did you do?'

'What did I do? I sprayed 'em with the washer. One of 'em stuck its backside against the windscreen and 'nissed all over the glass.'

'Why I can't believe it, the …'

'And then it just sat there on the fender showing its teeth and shmirking. I wanted to get out, me, and give the flamer a belt.'

With his spindly, white, bowed legs he struck up a pugilistic stance to illustrate and as the conversation ping-ponged across the chip shop and the queue stood in hushed concentration, I was suddenly aware of Lance stirring the chip pan without looking and the windows, all covered with pearly spots of rain on the outside, steaming grey on the in.

'Anyone for fish only?' sang Grace as she minced through the swish curtain with a tray of new made patties, whereupon Tom raised his hand like a little boy, skipped to the front and was served and off before he even had time to check his change.

'G'bye now and er … thank yer?' called Lance, weakly, before he turned to me. 'We get all sorts in ere,' he said, outdone, and with a solemn shake of his goaty grey beard, 'All sorts.'

And as I stepped out into the damp November evening and the cars swished by on the black shiny streets, I couldn't help thinking. 'Now wait a minute. How did he know there were *twenty-six* baboons? Did he count them? He was having us on! Anyway, what was he doing on "safari"? How did he get back?' And now I'd never know how it all ended. It's not always easy to just mind your own business though, is it?

'Six letters, it's a part of the eye and it ends in "i-n-a",' said my dad, leaving a blue stain on his tongue as he licked the end of his felt-tip to finish his *Sun* crossword.

'Vagina,' said my Uncle Kevin. 'V-e-g-i-n-a, there y'are, it fits.'

'It's retina,' I said, looking up from my writing. 'R-e-t-i-n-a. Retina is a part of the eye. Vagina is a part of a … woman. And it only fits because for "Papal residence" in four down you've put "caravan" instead of "Vatican".'

'Who asked you?' said my dad.

'Who do you think you are, Bob Holderness?' said my Uncle Kevin. 'We're not fick you know. I'm off to work.'

As Uncle Kevin's Mr Whippy ice-cream van pulled away to the chimes of the theme to *Lawrence of Arabia* my dad folded up his *Sun* and tucked it under his cushion. Maybe he was right. I should keep my big nose out.

'It'll get you into trouble one of these days,' he said ominously. 'You'll see.'

One cold Sunday I was standing at the back of a queue in the farm shop in Coniston with my own little boy, who has all the patience of a clockwork mouse. 'Put it back' I have to say before he licks the boiled sweet lolly he knows full well I'll then have to pay for. 'Put that down. No you can't have that, put it back!'

At the head of the line a rather large and marshmallow-complexioned lady was regaling the shop with tales of her virtues as a charity fund-raiser.

'And, of course the WI bazaar raised over £450 with the very generous donation of bric-a-brac from Lady Constable. And now ticket sales are picking up for the charity gun dog trial.'

'Dad,' said my little boy, tugging my shirt.

'No, son, not now,' I hissed, thinking that this was beginning to get interesting. 'But dad …'

'I don't suppose many of these wretched people have any concept of the sweat we pour on their behalf. No concept. I'm sure they think we just rattle a few tins on flag day and that's it.'

'Err …' interrupted the shopkeeper, 'Was it two eggs madam? Yes, of course errrrr …'

'A quarter of mushrooms, a salad onion and two ounces of that cheese,' she demanded.

He continued to put together her order as she spoke, twisting the corners of the brown paper bags into parcels and pencilling the prices on to a piece of newsprint next to his scales.

'That'll be one pound forty seven, please, errrr …'

'It'll have to be a cheque,' she snapped.

'Dad,' said my little boy, tugging at my trousers pockets. 'Dad.'

'No, son, not now,' I replied, not looking and locked now into the drama that was unfolding before us. I willed the shopkeeper to ask for her cheque guarantee card as she began to fill in the stub on her cheque book with great fat flourishes of her fountain pen, but all he did was smile his silly sheepish smile. I'd have made her sign something else, you know, just to verify her signature, or I might even have asked for further identification, preferably a letter or something with her address on.

'Anyway, I can't stand here letting you chat me up all day,' she called as she blustered towards the door, 'Or these people will think we're carrying on! Cheerio.'

'Heh, heh, thank you madam errrrr, turrah.'

There was a note of relief in the shopkeeper's bleaty voice as he giggled and called after her, but then she suddenly stopped in her tracks and turned back frostily towards him.

'Turrah?' 'she sneered. 'Turrah? Do I look like Cilla?'

'Dad.'

'No, son, not now.'

'Err,' bleated the shopkeeper, in his silly sheep voice.

'Dad, look,' said my son, holding up his finger towards me, 'I've got a bogey.'

'You naughty boy,' I said, as the audience turned its disapproving eyes towards me.

'Put it back.'

© 2006 Garry Burnett and Crown House Publishing Ltd – *Mrs Ockleton's Rainbow Kite and Other Tales: Thinking Through Literature*

SECTION 1 | **Twenty-six Baboons**

# 8 Twenty-six Baboons

## TEACHERS' NOTES

Pupils will have opportunities to attain at the following Key Stage 3 National Curriculum levels:

## En 2 (Reading)

Pupils will have opportunities to demonstrate reading skills at the following levels:

### At level 5a

a  To match talk to different situations
b  Use vocabulary precisely and organise communication clearly
c  Contribute, evaluate others' ideas, vary participation

### At level 6a

j  Express a personal response to texts with reference to language, structure and themes

I always view this story as a 'performance piece', one I use to 'end the show' in order to 'send the audience away with a smile'. I was once paid a huge compliment by a girl who had heard the CD recording and asked 'who did all of the other voices?' I actually concocted the 'eavesdropping' story theme following an excursion to the bar at the interval of *Les Miserables* in Manchester when my wife and I overheard two utterly convincing very upper class accents articulating complete nonsense about the performance they had just seen.

I was very conscious of not being over-descriptive in this piece, so the reader might note that it does rely heavily on internal and external dialogue, rather than detailed descriptions of characters and scene. The whole notion of 'internal' commentary is one I assimilated from the first person narrative persona Scout Finch in Harper Lee's *To Kill a Mockingbird* – the idea of the 'wise' child deconstructing the madness of the world around her really appealed to my own sense of perspective. Naturally I could have added much more but the humour, I think, is better contained and communicated in its brevity.

As a boy I was a fan of the comedian Les Dawson, and particularly of his two character creations the lecherous 'Cosmo Smallpiece' and the drunk 'Happy Harry Merryweather'. There is certainly something of Cosmo in the character of Tom. My friend Peter Thomas asks me to perform this story to his PGCE students at Hull University annually and then completely distracts me by laughing all the way through it. He says it's partly due to my gurning in the first section – I have obviously missed a vocation.

⊙ This story can be found on Track 4 of the audio CD accompanying this book.

# Twenty-six Baboons

**1** At the beginning of the story 'Twenty-six Baboons' is the following quote:

> The wedding guest sate on a stone
> He cannot chuse but hear
> And thus spake on that ancyent man
> The bright eyed Marinere
>
> SAMUEL COLERIDGE,
> *The Ryme of the Ancient Marinere*

Why do you think the author chose this quote to put at the beginning of the story? What is its connection?

**2** Why is 'Twenty-six Baboons' an appropriate title for this story? Can you think of an alternative title? Give your reasons for choosing it.

**3** The story is built around three different stories. What is their connection? How are they linked together?

Read the following extract from a newspaper story (*Daily Express*, August 3rd 2004).

## The grease monkeys

They appear to be the ideal car mechanics. Always enthusiastic and energetic, they work at speed and – unlike their human counterparts – it won't cost yer.

Unfortunately, motorists dropping their car off for a service at Longleat Safari Park should also be prepared to find their aerial missing and a part of their steering wheel chewed away.

So far there have been no complaints from irate drivers about the park's 80 rhesus monkeys. The only vehicle the primates have customised so far is a clapped out white Renault deliberately left at their mercy by the wardens.

The Keeper left the car as a plaything for the monkeys after noticing they appeared restless and depressed while they were starved of visitors during the foot and mouth crisis. Normally, the monkeys would be able to tamper with the windscreen wipers, wing mirrors and aerials of thousands of cars visiting their enclosure on Lord Bath's estate in Wiltshire.

Although the monkeys cannot catch foot and mouth disease, their home is in a section of the park closed to visitors because it contains animals which are vulnerable such as giraffes, elephants, camels and deer. Head warden Keith Harris said: 'It's obvious they are missing the opportunity to "interact" with visitors vehicles.

'Longleat is a huge estate and over the years we have inevitably accumulated a number of abandoned cars.

'Rather than scrapping them we thought we could use some of these vehicles to keep the monkeys happy until the real things return.'

Answer the following questions on the newspaper extract above.

**1** Why are the rhesus monkeys allowed to play on the cars and tear them apart?
**2** Comment on the use of the words 'interact' and 'customised' by the writer of the story.
**3** What evidence is there in the first paragraph of the attitude of the writer to the story?

Now answer these questions on the story 'Twenty-six Baboons'.

**1** 'Wait a minute, he was having us on!' says the author (about the old man in the fish and chip shop). Explain why you think he thinks this.
**2** Explain why the author says Lance, the chip-shop owner, felt 'outdone'?
**3** 'He continued to put together her order as she spoke, twisting the corners of the brown paper bags into parcels and pencilling the prices on to a piece of newsprint next to his scales.' The repetition of the letter 'p' in this extract is meant to add humour to the description of the events in the shop. This language device is called 'alliteration', that is, the repetition of letters in order to create a particular effect. Find other examples of alliteration in the story and comment on the effect they have.
**4** What is the funniest conversation you have ever heard? Transcribe it as accurately as possible in the form of a 'sketch'.
**5** Try taping a 'natural' conversation (that is, if possible without those being taped being aware of the fact) exactly as it sounds. Write it out, as accurately as possible, complete with all of the 'hmms' and 'ahs'. What are the problems with simply 'transcribing' conversations?
**6** Who is the funniest person you have ever met? Write a character description of them and an account of an incident when they were particularly amusing.

© 2006 Garry Burnett and Crown House Publishing Ltd – *Mrs Ockleton's Rainbow Kite and Other Tales: Thinking Through Literature*

# 9 Billy the Cat

> Well Toto, I guess we're not in Kansas any more.
>
> DOROTHY, *The Wizard of Oz*

When Mr Gilzean our careers teacher asked Brian Gavin, 'What do you want to do when you leave school?', he replied, 'Go home and have my tea.' No one laughed either, even when he tried to pretend afterwards that he'd meant it to be a joke. We knew he didn't really have a clue and, if truth were known, at eleven years old, neither did we. Our Terry wanted to be a spaceman, Uncle Kevin an Elvis impersonator, my brother an American soldier and I wanted to be … a crime-fighting super-hero.

I wanted to be Billy the Cat.

Oh you could keep your Batman, Superman, Flash and Spiderman; there was only one crime-fighting schoolboy *Beano* comic super-hero as far as I was concerned and that was Billy the Cat. When I think about it, Billy the Cat would probably be banned nowadays for health and safety reasons or political correctness or whatever. You see he was *really* an orphaned school boy whose parents had been circus acrobats and he spent his evenings, when his partially deaf aunt thought he was upstairs doing his homework, leaping gracefully about on the rooftops of the town where he lived, tracking down criminals and 'righting wrongs'. (I think that this was also his catchphrase.)

He used to wear this tight-fitting, all-black outfit and a shiny hard helmet with whisker-like radio antennae, and a visor to make him look more feline and which kept his real identity a secret. I *so* wanted to be like him I even created my own Billy the Cat outfit, which I used to play out in at the park or in the ten-foot at the back of my house. One of the most striking features of this was the olive-green plastic replica World War II German soldier's helmet into which I pierced dart-holes for cat's whiskers made from stubby spent matches. My 'utility cat-sack' was a customised school satchel (unfortunately not black either, but two shades of brown) filled with conkers and autumn berries for 'cat-missiles', all of which added further intrigue to my generally bizarre attire.

Each night I would slink off to the 'rocks' in East Park where I would leap fearlessly across one side to the other shouting 'I am a righter of wrongs', much to the bewilderment of the parents and kids who'd only come out to feed carrots and bread to the wallabies or peacocks in the animal enclosure nearby. I spent most of my time dodging 'parkies' at closing time or creeping about behind the ornamental rock gardens. It is a small wonder I wasn't arrested for looking or behaving suspiciously as I swung my 'yo-yo' cat claw around on its string, ready to disable any escaping handbag thief who happened to be running away across the grass.

When I finally grew out of it I was just so thankful no one had actually taken a photo of me dressed as Billy the Cat. I hoped that the whole embarrassing episode might quickly disappear into family folk-lore and later on I might be able to deny it or even pretend it was really my brother. But no, my mum and my sister have such photographic recall of the whole episode and between gales of uncontrollable laughter have described it to all of my subsequent friends and girlfriends in such intricate detail I have no doubt that an excellent artist's impression of me could probably be produced, if required.

Much to the relief of everybody, I'm sure, my next hero was none other than 'Jumping Jimmy', the comic strip Zulu centre forward who, at over eight feet tall could out-leap every defender in the football league and then break a hole in the opponent's net with one of his cannon-shot headers. And although he used to laugh at my pretend games and characters too, my Grandad Burnett told me how my dad and my Uncle Alf used to play Tarzan and Boy on the pavements of Mersey Street and had even taught their daft collie dog, Prince, to roll over when they said 'ongawa', so it must be in my genes.

And anyway even my 'Billy the Cat' and 'Jumping Jimmy' phases were nothing, *no nothing*, compared to the near legendary excesses of Douglas 'The Dog' Mennell.

I suppose I never knew him all that well because he was in Mr Spandler's class, but at lunch or play times when we all kicked the stuffing out of each other playing 'football' we would see 'Dog' trotting round and round the perimeter of the playground, on his own, pretending he was driving a bus.

'Ding, ding. All aboard,' he would call. 'Ffffrumm. Could all passengers have their tickets ready, please,' then indicate with a hand signal and pull out to continue his journey.

'Fffruuum,' he rasped. 'Hold tight …' and so on.

At other times he would crouch in a corner, pretending he was a juke-box and then make all the sounds and actions of a record being selected and played, including his own very tuneless rendition of the song. Nothing could make him stop once he'd started a song either and he would always go right through until he had even performed the fade-out at the end.

'Who do you think you are?' bawled Mr Gorman to him in a special assembly.

'Thir, Dog Mennell,' said Mennell, holding out his hand to shake Mr Gorman's.

His real name was Douglas Allman Richmond Barker Mennell, but following a 'freak' accident when he had lost his left eye and six of his front teeth, his ill-fitting dental plate slipped every time he tried to say his Christian name and it always came out as 'Dog'.

Apparently his bus fetish grew into a quite worrying obsession and rumour has it that at weekends or summer nights he would ride the East Yorkshire buses to the coast, sitting upstairs at the front so he could 'drive', only then to be ferried home in the small hours by an impatient and weary local policeman.

On Saturday mornings me and my friends were regulars at the ABC minors children's club at the Royalty cinema on Southcoates Lane where we would cheer big screen super-heroes like Superman, Batman, the Lone Ranger and Zorro as they performed death-defying feats, leading to cliff-hanging endings where the evil villain set a killer buzz-saw in motion or the approaching train turned the corner ready to mow down a pretty heroine tied to the track.

Every two or three weeks, Dog would be up on the stage at the interval receiving a prize from Uncle Vernon, the compere, for it supposedly being his birthday. Uncle Vernon had such a bad memory he could never remember who had been up from one week to the next.

The only time I was ever presented with anything was when I made over three hundred words from the letters in 'THUNDERBIRDS' and even then I came second to somebody who'd made over six thousand. I don't know who counted though – probably Auntie Vera, the ice-cream lady, who never gave you the right change.

But sometimes, in the darkened cinema, Dog Mennell, who was a regular attender, would whip out his glass eye, poke out his teeth on their dental plate and then swagger up and down the aisles shouting 'Esmerelda, get me some water' like Quasimodo, the Hunchback of Notre Dame.

Loads of kids screamed and ran for the exits because he looked far more frightening than anything we ever saw on the screen and that, I suppose, for him, was one of the major attractions for being there.

'If you can't stop that attention-seeking behaviour, boy,' said Mr Starkey, 'You can just leave this room, right now.' Little suspecting that Dog would then mount the sill and leave by the second floor window.

It soon became clear to us that the kind of attention Dog Mennell was seeking was beyond the capability of most teachers in our school to provide.

'Watch now as the "Man of Steel" soars to the library, like a speeding arrow,' he declared in his best American accent and then jumped. It's a good job the covered way broke his fall or he might have really hurt himself. You could see the relief on Mr Starkey's ashen face as the starfish-shaped boy, spread-eagled on the covered way roof twitched and lifted his head as he spat out bits of black gravel stuck to his lips.

Dog's 'Hunchback' impression became his own personal favourite and developed to such a gothic degree that he shocked Mrs Dunnachie into showering David Glover with her boiling coffee when he leapt out from behind a pillar shouting 'Sanctuary' at break.

Once a week in the autumn term a creaking 'Boddy's' coach delivered us to East Hull Baths, where those of us taking 'certificates' would be marshalled by a team of instructors in maroon cotton tracksuits holding clip-boards. One afternoon, towards the end of a session, we all looked up in anticipation as the large, white, podgy form of Dog Mennell minced out from his changing cubicle and sidled down towards the non-swimmers paddling about on their own at the shallow end.

© 2006 Garry Burnett and Crown House Publishing Ltd – *Mrs Ockleton's Rainbow Kite and Other Tales: Thinking Through Literature*

'Durrr dum,' he growled, from the upturned corner of his mouth. 'Durrr dum, durrr dum, dum dum …'

And then he dived in and bit this poor unsuspecting kid with his back to him right on his calf.

You can't blame Stephen Bass for grabbing him by his hair as Dog shook his leg in his jaws like a threshing shark on a feeding frenzy.

'Aaaaggghhh!' shouted Bassey. 'Get him off. Get him … off,' as he poked his fingers into Mennell's false eye and pulled with all his might.

'Everybody out of the water!' bawled Mr Dawson, pointing angrily to the bruise-coloured crescent of teeth marks on Bassey's leg. 'What were you trying to do?'

'Thir, I was onny having a laugh,' said Dog.

'I can't hear anybody laughing now though, can you?'

'Thir, I've lotht me eye,' said Dog.

Well! There we all stood, dripping, on the edge of the baths waiting for the water to stop rocking so we could locate and recover Douglas 'Jaws' Mennell's eye from the sloping bright blue tiled floor of the pool.

'I see it,' said Stephen Biggs, slipping in with all the confidence of Tarzan diving for pearls.

After what seemed like an age of waiting, Biggsy's hand surfaced from the pool like a periscope from a submarine, turning Dog Mennell's eye this way and that so that it seemed to inspect the now shivering line of boys.

'Is your mother *mental*?' yelled Mr Gorman to Dog in a special assembly the next day.

'No, thir.'

'Is your father *mental*?'

'No thir.'

'Then why are you *mental*?'

'I don't know, thir.'

'What do you think you'll do when you leave my school?' he shouted. (Go on, I dared, in my mind, say 'Go home and have my tea'.)

'I don't know, thir,' he replied.

Late one August towards the end of the school summer holidays when I was fifteen, my Uncle Kevin said he'd take me on a trip 'for some work experience' on his barge, 'The Water Rose'. From Cook's yard near the edge of the Humber, he would sail down the River Trent to Keadby and return with a load of sand or gravel to moor up a short way down the River Hull.

Considering his early ambitions nobody would ever have guessed that Uncle Kevin would end up a 'bargee'. On this particular trip he wore a pirate patch over one eye, though I'm not sure he really needed it, and in fact I'm almost certain he switched it to the other eye half way through the trip.

Out under big East Yorkshire skies into the wide open estuary we sailed. Out to where the Vikings must have passed, a thousand years ago, in their long boats on their way to York; out to join busy river traffic and pilot boats chugging towards deep channels; out to where my granddad George would have watched as his ship moved towards the open sea, for the last time, to join the doomed convoys heading across the Atlantic.

How strange to see the city from here. The ancient towers of Holy Trinity church next to King Billy's statue glittering gold in the evening sunlight; the pigeon-clattering wood yards at Sammy's Point where we sometimes played and Wilberforce's blackened statue peering out over Queen's Gardens, all looked so different … from here.

'Oh a-let-a-me be, bop sha-wah dah, bop sha-wa, your a-teddy bear …' sang Uncle Kevin as he guided The Water Rose along the Humber for about three hours to the Trent and we dropped anchor to wait for the river aiger and the evening tide moving in.

'You go down the galley and mek' us a bacon sandwich and a brew,' he ordered. 'And watch out for rats. They're gutsy little buggers. Two of 'em rolled a packet of biscuits off the bed last week and et 'um underneath. They'll sup your tea if you don't watch it.'

'Aye, aye,' I said.

The smell of diesel oil had soaked into the thick-sliced bread in waxed packets and economy bacon Uncle Kevin had brought as provisions for this trip. Even the milk, the teabags, the grey sheets, the brown, woollen blankets and the piles of dirty magazines next to the sponge mattress bed, all reeked of diesel oil so much I was frightened in case when I lit the tiny paraffin stove the whole boat would blow up.

'So what are you gonna do when you leave school next year?' said Uncle Kevin taking a big swig of his tea.

'I'm not sure. Staying on I think.'

'I can allus get you a job on barges, wi me,' he said.

'No, thanks,' I said. 'I want to be … a writer.' ('Of wrongs' I felt like adding.)

'A writer!' he said, pausing to chew the almost raw, fatty bacon hanging over the edge of his sandwich like a tongue. 'Can you spell "Constantinople"?'

'Yes,' I said.

'Aye,' he said, raising his eyebrows and taking a big bite so that tomato sauce and bacon grease squeezed out of the sides and glistened like blood on his chin. 'So can I.'

In the flickering half-light of the paraffin lamp, Uncle Kevin blinked his good eye like Cyclops squatting at the edge of his cave and continued to devour his doorstep-sized bacon sandwich with big tearing bites. Behind him on the cabin bed a discarded sock twitched and a small, brown, whiskery face, stuffed with bread and bacon, blinked a beady black eye as it peeped around a fold in the blanket.

'Pah,' he said. 'Anyway, what are you gonna write about?'

There was a sharp squeak as Uncle Kevin lobbed a cranking iron at the moving lump on the bunk.

'Stories,' I said. 'You know, about things that have happened … to me.'

'You?' sneered Uncle Kevin.

'Oh yeh. Like what?' he scoffed, as outside the river aiger lapped against the rocking, rolling barge, the evening tide swelled and the water rose.

## Vocabulary

**Aiger**    a tidal wave

**Ten-foot**    a small alley, an area between houses where garages usually project into and often used by children as a play area – often not more than 'ten-foot' in width

© 2006 Garry Burnett and Crown House Publishing Ltd – *Mrs Ockleton's Rainbow Kite and Other Tales: Thinking Through Literature*

# 9 Billy the Cat
## TEACHERS' NOTES

Pupils will have opportunities to attain at the following Key Stage 3 National Curriculum levels:

### En 2 (Reading)

Pupils will have opportunities to demonstrate reading skills at the following levels:

#### At level 5a

a   To show understanding
    Develop inference
    Select appropriate evidence
d   Understand how texts are organised (and use similar organisational strategies in own work)
f   Discuss the degree of success the author has achieved literary objectives

#### At level 6a

g   Read and discuss a wide range of texts
h   Identify *layers* of meaning
i   Identify the effects and significance of texts
j   Express a personal response to texts with reference to language, structure and themes

#### At level 7a

k   Select and synthesise information

### En3 (Writing)

Pupils will have opportunities to demonstrate writing skills at the following levels:

#### At level 6a

a   To write to engage the reader's interest
b   To use appropriate form and structure

#### At level 7a

c   Show clear sense of purpose and audience

I was interested here in exploring 'what makes a story' and I suppose, through the extract 'Tell your story Thomas Leaf' on page 91, 'what makes a good storyteller?'. Is it simply having an interesting, funny or engaging story to tell or are there other factors involved connected with sensitivity to moment, person and place? The political correctness of the middle tale is something I obviously had personal problems with – and I couldn't help feeling the same sense of responsibility Alan Bleasdale felt when he wrote *Yosser's Tale*, or Alan Bennett with Miss Shepherd in *The Lady in the Van*.

What connects the three tales is I suppose the sense of identity and the growth towards Maslow's sense of self-actualisation 'Who do you think you *are*?' or 'Who do you want *to be*?' or 'Who do you hope *to become*?'. In my own case it was 'becoming' a writer, with all of the attendant challenges of circumstance, class, self-doubt and identity crisis. Drawing upon material from life and family is one that is fraught with dangers for the writer – the biggest one being that great offence might be given to someone you actually care a lot about.

The activity 'Inventing a new comic super-hero' allows pupils free reign of the imagination. Perhaps the more gifted can grasp the deeper 'ironies' in order to attempt spoof characters (for example, Mr Incredible, the Batman TV series).

Prior to using the activity 'Creative writing: tell your story …', pupils may be asked to bring in a snapshot image from their childhood to prompt their own creative writing.

# Favourite super-hero

**'Billy the Cat' and 'Katie the Cat'**

| | |
|---|---|
| Real names | Billy – William Grange |
| | Katie – Kathleen Grange |
| Identity/class | Unknown – human mutants? |
| Occupation | School kids |
| Enemies | All criminals |
| Known relatives | Aunt Mabel |
| Aliases | None |
| Base of operations | Burnham |
| Powers/abilities | Both Billy and Katie have identical abilities. They are incredibly agile, able to leap superhuman distances, somersault and dodge around with para-human grace. They appear to be somewhat stronger than average, as for a pair of children they seem strong enough to fight adults and Katie is strong enough to hold the weight of a falling child of her own size at the end of a rope without much strain. They have excellent balance, running and jumping from one rooftop to another, and can climb sheer surfaces without difficulty. They seem to have above normal stamina and can adventure all night and still manage to handle school without the slightest sign of being tired. They can swim underwater for great distances without coming up for breath while wearing leather catsuits and crash helmets and appear to handle extreme temperatures as well, also while wearing tight black leather. Each uses a weighted nylon line to lasso things, a line which is strong enough to tie up an adult criminal and support the weight of a child. |
| History | Schoolboy William Grange had lived with his Aunt Mabel since the day his parents, both of whom worked for the police, were killed in a car crash caused by the getaway car of a group of bank robbers. As a result, William vowed to use his amazing abilities to fight crime, as the heroic Billy the Cat! His amazing gear had been made for him from designs created by his father, a clever inventor. |
| Costumes | Their costumes consist of black leather catsuits, with black backpacks (which at a guess hold their civilian clothes) attached by leather straps. They wear crash helmets, modified to look like a cat's face, to hide their identities. Since Katie wears a short skirt as a part of her school uniform, the two must keep their costumes hidden in their school bags, because on at least one occasion they switch identities in an alley on the way home from school. |

1 'Well Toto, we're not in Kansas anymore' (from the *Wizard of Oz*). Why do you think the writer begins the story with this quote?
2 Explain why Billy the Cat was the writer's all-time super-hero.
3 Who is your favourite 'super-hero'? Give reasons for your choice.

© 2006 Garry Burnett and Crown House Publishing Ltd – *Mrs Ockleton's Rainbow Kite and Other Tales: Thinking Through Literature*

# Inventing a new comic super-hero (1)

Now create a super-hero of your own, using the activity sheet 'Inventing a new comic super-hero (2)' to structure your ideas.

**Drawing of my super-hero**

© 2006 Garry Burnett and Crown House Publishing Ltd – *Mrs Ockleton's Rainbow Kite and Other Tales: Thinking Through Literature*

SECTION 1 | **Billy the Cat**

# Inventing a new comic super-hero (2)

Real name

Identity

Costumes


Occupation

Enemies


Known relatives


Aliases


Base of operations




Powers/abilities





History




When you have done this, write ideas for the 'pilot' first episode to launch your character. It can be in a comic or magazine of your choice.

# Back to the story …

**1** Once again the writer has used the 'three-stories within a story' structure. How does he make them connect together? How well does it work?

**2** The writer uses several 'puns' in the story. 'Puns' are plays on words, sometimes to make a joke. For example:

> Sherlock Holmes was painting his door yellow when Dr Watson called around. 'Why are you doing that Holmes?' To which Holmes replies 'It's a lemon entry, my dear Watson.' (Sherlock Holmes often used the phrase 'It's elementary my dear Watson.')

Share any jokes you know with puns in them.

**3** Find three examples of puns in the story. Explain how the writer uses them to create a comic effect.

1

2

3

**4** Why do you think the story ends on Uncle Kevin's barge, the way it does?

© 2006 Garry Burnett and Crown House Publishing Ltd – *Mrs Ockleton's Rainbow Kite and Other Tales: Thinking Through Literature*

SECTION 1 | **Billy the Cat**

# Broken Roots (1)

In the following poem the writer recalls a series of images and events from his past.

## Broken Roots

Moving through the garden, brooding, trowel held like
a weapon, I find a frail plant struggling in
a bleak and sunless corner. Kneeling to prise
it up the clod comes away and lies cold in
my pale palm. Broken roots trail, tremble in air
they've never known, and in the garden's silence
I recall how I was shifted from town to town,
Uprooted, made to feel strange in strange places.

The memory camera whirrs its old movies,
stuttering images glut and blur behind
my eyes. Men in battered hats fork hay, sirens
wail down a long street, a woman bleeds beneath
a tram, on a strand wind whips sand into young
faces, hens scutter in a kitchen's darkness.
But to this there is no geography, no map
to read. Forgotten landscapes fade to greyness.

I fish for faces, dredge up fixed smiles which gaze
from ageing snapshots. I track my blood line back
through the years but the trail dries up, there are no
more people. I find no reason for being in
this silent place, and kneeling here on the damp
earth I come to a dead end. I stare at my
clenched fist. The frail plant, its roots, are crushed.
The clod crumbles, soil dribbles through my fingers
like days, days.

WES MAGEE

1 Discuss together the sequence of events and the thoughts the man has as he walks in the garden. What actually happens in the poem? Tell the story of his walk.

2 Pick three particular words, phrases or descriptions in the poem that stand out in your mind. Write them down and explain your reasons for choosing them.

3 Sometimes writers use 'metaphors' to express or describe things (a metaphor can be *another way* of saying something, for example, Shakespeare once wrote 'All the world's a stage…'). How do you think the poet uses a 'plant' and 'trailing roots' in this poem as a metaphor for his life?

4 What are the feelings the poet expresses in this poem? Back up your ideas with examples of his language.

5 'The memory camera whirrs its old movies…' Imagine you are going to produce a video to accompany the poem. Use the blank storyboard sheet 'Broken Roots (2)' to plan a series of images you would film.

# Broken Roots (2)

| Image | Words |
|-------|-------|
|       |       |
|       |       |
|       |       |
|       |       |
|       |       |
|       |       |
|       |       |

© 2006 Garry Burnett and Crown House Publishing Ltd – *Mrs Ockleton's Rainbow Kite and Other Tales: Thinking Through Literature*

SECTION 1 | **Billy the Cat**

# 'Tell your story Thomas Leaf'

Some people possess extremely good interpersonal and linguistic intelligence and can communicate to others very powerfully and effectively, especially when they are telling a story. Others can't! Read this attempt to enthral an audience by the frustrated storyteller Thomas Leaf.

Towards the end of Thomas Hardy's novel *Under the Greenwood Tree* one of the rustic characters, a simpleton called Thomas Leaf, is encouraged to tell a story to his group of friends from the Mellstock Choir.

'Let's hear thy story, Leaf' said the **tranter**. 'I never knew you were clever enough to tell a story. Silence, all of ye! Mr Leaf will tell a story.'

'Tell your story Thomas Leaf,' said grandfather William in the tone of a schoolmaster.

'Once,' said the delighted Leaf, in an uncertain voice, 'there was a man who lived in a house! Well, this man went thinking and thinking night and day. At last, he said to himself, as I might, "If I had only ten pounds, I'd make a fortune." At last by hook or by crook, behold he got the ten pounds!'

'Only think of that!' said Nat Callcome satirically.

'Silence!' said the tranter.

'Well, now comes the interesting part of the story! In a little time he made that ten pounds twenty. Then a little time after that he doubled it, and made it forty. Well he went on, and a good while after that he made it eighty, and on to a hundred. Well, by-and-by he made it two hundred! Well, you'd never believe it, but – he went on and made it four hundred! He went on, and what did he do? Why, he made it eight hundred! Yes he did' continued Leaf in the highest pitch of excitement, bringing down his fist upon his knee with such force that he quivered with pain; 'yes, and he went on and made it a THOUSAND!'

'Hear, hear!' said the tranter. 'Better than the history of England, my sonnies!'

'Thank you for thy story, Thomas Leaf,' said Grandfather William; and then Leaf gradually sank into nothingness again.

## Thinking about 'the story'

1 How does the tranter build up our expectations for Leaf's story?

2 What is disappointing about it?

3 How does Hardy make the description of the episode funny?

4 What do you think are the qualities that make a story a 'good' story?

5 What advice would you give Leaf for making his stories more enjoyable?

6 Write a story of no more than 250 words, in the style of Thomas Leaf's, in which you try to make something sound interesting which is in fact quite boring and ordinary. For example, having your breakfast, brushing your teeth, cleaning your shoes, walking to school.

## Vocabulary

**Tranter**     transporter – a kind of delivery man

© 2006 Garry Burnett and Crown House Publishing Ltd – *Mrs Ockleton's Rainbow Kite and Other Tales: Thinking Through Literature*

# Have something interesting to say…?

'Pah,' he said. 'Anyway, what are you gonna write about?'

There was a sharp squeak as Uncle Kevin lobbed a cranking iron at the moving lump on the bunk.

'Stories,' I said. 'You know, about things that have happened … to me.'

'You?' sneered Uncle Kevin.

'Oh yeh. Like what?' he scoffed, as outside the river aiger lapped against the rocking, rolling barge, the evening tide swelled and the water rose.

(from 'Billy the Cat')

## Jack and the Storytelling Contest

Every year the village held a storytelling contest at the inn on the edge of the lake. And everyone would gather to drink the strong beer, eat the delicious food and listen to the marvellous storytellers who came from all over the county to thrill the audience with their tales of magic and mystery and strange and wonderful deeds.

The villagers would fill their plates and gather, wide-eyed around the large fire to listen to them compete for the two main trophies which were:

A large bottle of whisky for the best story

A large bottle of brandy for the best *lie*

It was a tradition of the evening for the compere to ask an unprepared member of the audience to stand up to tell a story. But if they refused, they were ordered to pay a forfeit, which usually consisted of some menial, humiliating task – either that or pay a fine and leave the room!

Each year Jack, a shy bachelor who lived on his father's isolated farm, would creep quietly into the back of the room hoping not to be noticed and secretly wish that he too could be like the great storytellers. He knew though that this was very unlikely for he led such an uneventful life and had very little to tell stories about.

One year when he arrived at the contest a little later than usual the compere saw him trying to sneak in and asked in a very loud voice, 'You there at the back?'

'Who? Me?' answered Jack, his heart beating like a frog.

'Yes, you. Come on lad, stand up and give us all a story.'

'Oh, er, goodness me,' mumbled Jack. 'I don't know any' and he suddenly felt extremely foolish as all eyes turned to him.

'Then you must pay a forfeit,' answered the compere. 'Hmm. Now what shall it be? At the edge of the lake you will find a small fishing boat which has been pulled up high on to the shore. Take this copper scoop and empty it of all water. And don't come back until you have finished!'

Jack closed the door to sniggers from the others in the audience and stepped out into the frosty evening air. 'I shall always be alone! Who'd ever be interested in me?' he cried.

As Jack climbed into the boat and reached into his red waistcoat pocket for his small clay pipe, suddenly the boat was pulled, as if by an unseen force, into the centre of the lake, flinging him back and knocking him out cold.

Several hours must have passed because when he woke it was daylight and when he looked around he saw none of the familiar sights around him he knew so well. In fact things looked very strange indeed. It was while he was looking that he happened to glance at his hands and instead of the red, callused hands of a labourer, he saw the pale delicate hands of a young woman. And when Jack looked at his feet, instead of the heavy working boots he had worn previously, there were pretty, feminine shoes covering his very feminine feet.

Glancing over the edge of the boat, Jack examined his reflection in the lake. He saw now that his appearance had been completely transformed and to all intents and purposes he was a woman.

'Can I help you?' said a voice suddenly, as Jack began to sob into his hands.

(continued)

---

© 2006 Garry Burnett and Crown House Publishing Ltd – *Mrs Ockleton's Rainbow Kite and Other Tales: Thinking Through Literature*

SECTION 1 | **Billy the Cat**

# Have something interesting to say…? (contd.)

He looked up to see a handsome young man gazing with obvious concern back at him. Not wishing to appear foolish, Jack muttered something about 'memory' and 'bang on the head', so the young man invited Jack back to his mother's cottage where he was greeted with great hospitality. In fact the young man seemed very interested in Jack and over the course of the next few days they became quite good friends.

As Jack began to get used to his transformation he decided that things weren't in fact all that bad after all and, actually, as a woman he was quite an attractive person, with lots of new friends and admirers. The young man's mother cared for Jack as if he were her own daughter and it wasn't long before the young man was proposing marriage. His previous life as a farm labourer now seemed little more than a distant memory and Jack settled into married life comfortably and quickly. After a year, the couple had a son and one year later a daughter and Jack was as content as he could have wished to be.

One evening, several years later, however, Jack was walking alone by the edge of the lake when over in the reeds he caught sight of something which seemed strangely familiar and he walked down to take a closer look. It was a boat and on its floor he saw a small clay pipe and next to it a bright copper scoop. As he bent to pick it up, the boat was suddenly pulled, as if by an unseen hand, towards the centre of the lake and Jack was flung back and knocked unconscious by its force.

When he awoke it was dark and the stars twinkled like frost in the sky. He looked down at his hands, his feet and his body. Gone were the pretty clothes, the shoes, the pale delicate skin and in its place he saw the coarse grimy hands, the denim shirt and red waistcoat he had worn all those years before.

He leapt from the boat and ran up to the inn at the side of the lake where the storytelling competition was still underway. As he burst through the door, the voices were suddenly silent and all eyes turned to him as he shouted 'Where's my husband? Where are my children?'

'Hold on a minute,' said the compere, struggling not to smile, 'Jack, tell us what's troubling you.'

And when Jack had finished telling his story, the compere raised his eyebrows and shook his head.

'Well son,' he said, pausing for effect, 'That was not only the best story we have heard this evening, it has got to be the biggest lie.'

And although Jack took home the bottle of whisky and the bottle of brandy that night, I'm not sure he went home a happy man.

GARRY BURNETT<br>(based on a traditional tale)

1  What is the message to potential storytellers in this story?

2  What do you think Jack learns from the whole storytelling episode?

3  Would you say the story had a 'happy' or a 'sad' ending? Give reasons for your opinion.

4  After reading the extracts in this section and 'Billy the Cat' do you think a good story has to be based on a dramatic, funny or shocking event?

# Creative writing: tell your story …

*Mrs Ockleton's Rainbow Kite and Other Tales* is a collection of stories all of which were inspired by actual incidents and people. Many writers have been inspired by *personal* memories and encounters with people.

Using the photograph you have brought into this lesson as inspiration, write a memory poem of your own.

The photograph may have a *story behind it*, perhaps you could tell the story.

It may be a *character*, *friend* or *relative*. Perhaps you could describe them in detail and some of the important memories you have of them.

It may be about a *place* or *time* that has a special importance to you. Perhaps you could describe the place or time in detail in order to bring the memory alive for others.

Remember to always plan your ideas for writing before you begin in order to give your work structure (use the box below or a separate sheet of paper).

> **Notes**

# A chapter from my autobiography

You will now have the chance to write about an episode from your life.

Imagine that this will form a chapter from your forthcoming autobiography and will be published to promote the book in a teenage magazine.

Give this 'chapter' a title. It could be from any stage of your life 'the primary school years' or 'first holiday abroad' for example, or it could be based on something quite recent.

Try to make this chapter as entertaining and interesting as possible (after all you want them to want to read the rest of the story!) and aim it at an audience of readers of your own age.

© 2006 Garry Burnett and Crown House Publishing Ltd – *Mrs Ockleton's Rainbow Kite and Other Tales: Thinking Through Literature*

SECTION 1 | **Billy the Cat**

# 10 Mrs Ockleton's Rainbow Kite

© 2006 Garry Burnett and Crown House Publishing Ltd – *Mrs Ockleton's Rainbow Kite and Other Tales: Thinking Through Literature*

**Mrs Ockleton's Rainbow Kite** | SECTION 1

> 'Pah,' he said. 'Anyway, what are you gonna write about?'
> 'Stories,' I said. 'You know, about things that have happened … to me.'
> 'You?' sneered Uncle Kevin. 'Oh yeh. Like what?'
>
> GARRY BURNETT, 'Billy the Cat'

Mrs Ockleton's son was an inventor.

He had all sorts of brilliant ideas for extraordinary inventions. Some of which were very clever and useful. Some of which, it must be said, didn't work as well as he had hoped.

For example, the general public never forgot the 'Ockleton Pre-Programmable Dancing Shoes' fiasco. Or the numerous court cases surrounding the 'Ockleton Pre-Programmable Auto Hair-Styling Helmet' charade.

'I don't know where he gets it from,' said Mrs Ockleton, turning the pages of her scrapbook, 'It must be his father. I'm a complete dunce, especially when it comes to new ideas.'

But if Mrs Ockleton were ever to go on *Mastermind*, her specialist subject would be 'old films'. Though sometimes she couldn't call to mind exact details, if you know what I mean.

One windy day in March, Mrs Ockleton was sitting in her comfortable armchair, knitting a long, multi-coloured scarf. She was waiting for the old film to start on the television and leaned forward to pick up a brightly coloured ball of wool which had slipped from her lap.

'Mother you'll never guess what!' came an excited shout from the hall. 'I've done it this time. I've just finished something that will revolutionise personal transportation, solve the world energy crisis, end global warming and provide hours of low-cost fun for all the family. You've got to come and see.'

And taking his mother by the arm, Mrs Ockleton's son led her to the garden outside.

'Well, it's a beautiful colour, love, but what is it? And what does it do?'

Shaped like a giant arrowhead on the lawn was a large multi-coloured kite. A lawnmower-sized engine fastened to its under-carriage drove an eight-blade propeller. A person-shaped harness hung to the crossbars.

'There are still one or two minor adjustments to be made,' he said. 'And of course this is only the prototype "recreational" model. It can carry a person who weighs seven stones or less and I've called it "The Ockleton Rainbow Kite".'

'And what sort of a fool do you think you'd get to go in that?' she said, shaking her head.

'Ah,' said Mrs Ockleton's son, 'I was coming to that …'

'Mrs Ockleton to mission control,' said Mrs Ockleton, with a wink to the growing assembly of spectators as she adjusted the radio microphone on her specially customised safety helmet and clipped the safety cord to the weight-lifter's belt around her waist.

'Receiving you loud and clear,' he replied.

And then, before she had time to even think twice about this most marvellous adventure, the Rainbow Kite was filled and tugged by a sudden sharp gust of wind and, like a skylark rising full sail into the bright blue morning sky, Mrs Ockleton flew.

'It's a beautiful view,' she said to her son (when she finally opened her eyes) as the Rainbow Kite rocked from side to side like a conductor's baton high above the gardens and ten-foots and chimneys of Sunny Bank.

'And I can see your house from up here.'

Mrs Ockleton remained remarkably calm. She'd always been a martyr to her feet, but just lately she'd not been able to get around much at all.

'Way above the chimney pots that's where you'll find me!' sang Mrs Ockleton as the Rainbow Kite pulled dangerously at the safety line.

'Now which fillum did that come from?' she wondered as she waved to the growing crowd below. 'It's on the tip of my blooming tongue.'

Looking a little bit like a baby at the end of a long umbilical cord, Mrs Ockleton bobbed and fluttered and danced above the spectators congregated on Mother Earth until another sudden strong gust of wind stretched the safety string until it strained and snapped and, slowly at first, across the sky the Rainbow Kite began to move.

© 2006 Garry Burnett and Crown House Publishing Ltd – *Mrs Ockleton's Rainbow Kite and Other Tales: Thinking Through Literature*

'You've no need to worry, mother,' was the last thing she heard her son say as he pressed every button on the control handset, though it never struck Mrs Ockleton how when radio contact was lost, voices continued to crackle in the earpiece of her headset.

'There's no place like home,' whispered one, as the Rainbow Kite drifted silently over the streets and houses she knew so well.

'Keep calm,' said another. 'Something *wonderful* will happen.'

Then, as she peered down from a great height on the fish docks and tall cranes at the edge of the Humber, the Rainbow Kite turned purposefully to point towards the sun and, as if it had a mind of its own, began to steadily pick up speed.

'And finally,' concluded a well-known newsreader with a smirky, half-grin on his face, as he ended a particularly depressing bulletin, 'We are receiving unusual reports of a missing person. Eighty-six-year-old Dorothy Ockleton of Minnie's Grove, Hull disappeared today after the large kite she was strapped to broke free and soared into the upper atmosphere. In an interview this evening her son said "She's never done this sort of thing before. She usually stays in most afternoons to watch old films."'

Then the newscaster began to laugh (rather disrespectfully, some thought) so uncontrollably at the thought of old Mrs Ockleton whooping and diving in the clouds, that the clip was shown on *It'll be Alright on the Night* for years to come.

Hourly bulletins featured amateur video footage of the Rainbow Kite over many well-known British landmarks. Air traffic control were still 'playing it by ear', as nobody knew exactly what the kite might do, or where it might go next.

But the general public was gripped. 'Ockleton-spotting' suddenly became a national pastime and after the TV weather report in the evening there was to be a special 'Ockleton update' speculating on where she might be seen the following day.

The pigeons of Trafalgar Square flew neatly in formation behind the Rainbow Kite, creating a giant, rude-looking V-sign in the sky behind the Lord Mayor as he posed for his re-election campaign photographs. Mr Livingstone, not known to be a pigeon-fancier, was ever so embarrassed.

'The Hand of God' was the headline in the evening paper.

'Bravo!' shouted important guests at a special Buckingham Palace garden party, who thought Mrs Ockleton's fly-past was a part of the organised programme of entertainment (just before the fireworks). Her Majesty the Queen, with customary dignity, waved casually as if it was. Then she secretly motioned her manservant to make a note of the old lady's name and address in anticipation of her birthday honours list.

'We are *most* amused,' quipped the Queen, who, after all, needed a bit of cheering up herself.

Meanwhile, Mrs Ockleton, leaving the smoky city far behind her, soared like a bluebird over the white cliffs of Dover.

'Do you know I've lost all track of time,' said Mrs Ockleton. 'And I'll bet I've missed the start of that fillum now, *Jesus of Nazareth*. Never mind, I've seen it before. He dies in the end.'

'All this fresh air's done my sinuses no end of good. I haven't coughed once,' she said as she darted like a swift around the towers of Notre Dame.

'Est-ce qu'un oiseau? Est-ce qu'un avion? Mais, non, c'est Mme Ockleton' was the headline in *Le Figaro*.

And all this time Mrs Ockleton had no idea of her newly acquired international celebrity status. Back home offers of endorsements and sponsors poured in and made a pile on her mat, blocking the front door.

The only dirt the paparazzi could unearth related to overdue library books in 1967. So they didn't bother.

Age Concern was especially concerned when sightings of the Rainbow Kite were made over the Alps. They needn't have been – she was having a grand old time.

As she reached the Vatican City, the Pope said a special mass as she flew over St Peter's Square and thousands of people prayed that St Christopher would keep her safe. Mrs Ockleton had always wanted to visit Rome. Ever since she saw Kirk Douglas in *Spartacus*.

The Ancient Greeks would probably have thought Mrs Ockleton was a messenger from the Gods – either that or one of Zeus's winged harpies. Plane spotters in Athens just stood open mouthed as she circled the Parthenon. Nothing resembling a Rainbow Kite existed in their Observer's guides.

The Sultan of Oman was so impressed he ordered 200 Rainbow Kites as presents for his palace staff and family, and commissioned a specially adapted one to be made for himself, with gold-leaf decoration. Such was the extent of his admiration he even sent up his private jet to trail a banner with a proposal of marriage to Mrs Ockleton.

'It'd be like that fillum *The Sheik* starring, what's-his-name in his hareem and me riding the camel. No, thank you,' she declined graciously, 'I'd look a complete radish in a veil.'

And, adjusting her customised Japanese sniper helmet, which made her look a little bit like Deputy Dawg, she steered the kite east, towards the lands of the rising sun.

At a special debate in the United Nations, the assembled governments of the world all agreed that Mrs Ockleton should be allowed to fly freely through their air space. After all, no one wanted to appear to be a 'meanie'. Seeing as it was the first thing they had ever all agreed on, they celebrated the occasion by holding a very expensive party. 'We must agree more often,' they agreed.

Meanwhile, high above the billowing clouds, the Rainbow Kite tumbled and turned like a burnt paper scrap in a chimney flue.

'Oh look there's that nice Mr Branson in his balloon. You ought to get yourself one of these,' she said, twisting like a swallow. 'They don't half go.'

'But just how do we get her down?' asked the Prime Minister of Great Britain, showing sincere concern.

'Ah,' said Mrs Ockleton's son, 'I was coming to that …'

Still, given the choice, Mrs Ockleton would have stayed where she was (thank you very much). She had always dreamed of travelling, you see. But never like *this*.

High on a hillside in Afghanistan some ragged children stood up from their campfires to wave burning torches. Down in the streets of Bethlehem people even stopped fighting and looked up together towards the sky. Forgetting to be angry at each other for a while, they all joined to wave to Mrs Ockleton as she soared by like a shooting star. And afterwards they found they couldn't remember what they had been so angry about in the first place.

Air Qantas passengers were astonished to see an old lady passing them in a blur of colour as if they were standing still.

'This must be what they call 'G' force,' said Mrs Ockleton (with great difficulty) her hand held out, considerately, indicating she wished to overtake. 'I hope these teeth stay in alright.'

And the pilot, who had somehow missed all of the extensive media coverage, reported a UFO to air-traffic control.

'Unbelievable Flying Ockleton' was the headline for a lead story in the newspapers the next day.

And people were warned not to be alarmed when they saw an old lady strapped to a kite moving over the sky – it was only Mrs Ockleton, aviator, mother of the now famous inventor, and resident of Minnie's Grove, Hull.

It was also reported that Mrs Ockleton was on course to break the world record for a non-stop solo flight. If only she had known. She would have been so proud. Her mother had once served Amy Johnson in her fish and chip shop.

Children all over the world begged their parents to buy them a Rainbow Kite. Father Christmas received sacks full of letters that year, all asking for the same thing. It looked as if Mrs Ockleton's son would finally be famous for an invention that actually worked – something *he* had always dreamed of.

In secret meetings at the Ministry of Defence important men and women discussed the potential military application of Rainbow Kites.

'I hope that son of mine's remembered to take the pan off the cooker,' said Mrs Ockleton, thinking out loud.

© 2006 Garry Burnett and Crown House Publishing Ltd – *Mrs Ockleton's Rainbow Kite and Other Tales: Thinking Through Literature*

SECTION 1 | **Mrs Ockleton's Rainbow Kite**

The press descended on Minnie's Grove like a pack of hungry foxes. Archive photographs of Mrs Ockleton were few and far between. In fact the only recent one they could buy was taken just after the unsuccessful 'Auto Hair-Styling Helmet' trials, when the *Yorkshire Post*, much against her wishes, printed a photograph of Mrs Ockleton next to that of a gargoyle on York Minster and held a 'spot-the-difference' competition. That was an 'annus horribilus' and a half for the Ockletons, I can tell you.

Now everywhere she flew, people waved and smiled when they looked up to the sky and saw her. 'I'm filling up,' she sniffed, as some people even held up their babies.

High on a remote mountainside in Tibet, a family of Yetis threw snowballs at the brightly coloured bird creature gliding low above the Himalayas, growling and baring their large yellow teeth. So Mrs Ockleton did the same. Only she took hers completely out of her mouth. And away they ran.

Strong rumours began to circulate that Mrs Ockleton had been abducted by aliens. The tabloid newspapers had a field day! But to tell the truth, the aliens were too frightened by what they saw. They just turned their space ships around and headed back to their home planet, with tales of strange flying creatures patrolling the atmosphere.

And as a result, all plans for a full-scale invasion of Earth were cancelled.

Over in the east dark clouds gathered like the great ribbed underbelly of a giant fish, while coppery vapour trails criss-crossed the sky like soft fireworks to ripples of gentle thunder.

'Oh, it's so beautiful,' she said searching poetically for just the right words as she glided over the cloud field below. 'Like … mashed potato. Great big lumpy mashed potato.'

'I must be seeing things,' she gasped, wiping her safety goggles, as schools of dolphins and killer whales rose and splashed in the clouds above Hiroshima.

'There must be a hundred more kites down there, just like this one.'

It was as if a thousand suns had burst in the brilliant white light of morning and the sea and sky glittered like a field full of stars and Mrs Ockleton felt the thrill of great speed as the Rainbow Kite hurried across oceans and deserts, canyons and forests, fields and farms while the ground disappeared like a spinning treadmill beneath her.

But she never once felt afraid. Somehow she knew that all would be well.

As the dust clouds above Manhattan parted in the early spring sunshine some people swore they saw an angel with brightly coloured wings poised over the blasted ruins of the collapsed towers. Those who were religious remembered God's promise to Noah after the flood – that he would set a rainbow in the clouds as a sign of hope for better times to come. And for the first time since the darkest winter anyone could remember, their spirits lifted as they raised their eyes to the sky – and their hearts sang.

It was as if an invisible hand was guiding the Rainbow Kite as it turned to head south. Over mountains and rivers, prairies and pastures the kite continued its journey and Mrs Ockleton saw many strange and wonderful sights.

Until in the skies above Kansas she noticed a great heaving black column crackling and spinning like a top from the edge of the horizon to the clouds.

'Oh dear,' was all she could say, as she felt the kite drawn towards it as if by some unseen magnetic force.

It was a tornado, sometimes known as a *twister*.

The twister cut a line through fields and farms like hot water poured on snow, making an almighty noise as it rumbled near.

'Oh my,' she cried, squeezing her eyes tight shut as the mighty, roaring whirling monster sucked the tiny Rainbow Kite from the sky and into its great rippling belly.

Once inside she opened her eyes and to her surprise all was still.

The black walls of the tornado spun around her like the inside of a tumble drier while she hung suspended on the kite in the middle of the dark vertical tunnel.

'What now?' said Mrs Ockleton in a hushed voice.

© 2006 Garry Burnett and Crown House Publishing Ltd – *Mrs Ockleton's Rainbow Kite and Other Tales: Thinking Through Literature*

When, to her surprise, from out of the swirling column a little girl stepped into a sudden blade of bright white light.

'Hello,' said Mrs Ockleton and even though the little girl was strangely familiar she asked, 'What's your name?'

'Dorothy,' replied the little girl politely.

'Dorothy?' said Mrs Ockleton, 'Why, that's my name.'

'We're off to see the wizard,' whispered the little girl, looking around as if she was sharing a big important secret. Then she stepped back into the shadows.

'Are we now?' said Mrs Ockleton, a little puzzled. 'Don't I know you?'

But the little girl just smiled mysteriously and, before she could speak again, Mrs Ockleton felt the Rainbow Kite rise slowly towards a gaping hole in the sky where the great wheeling constellations of the Milky Way twinkled and shone like sprinkles of bright winter frost.

'Space …' she said, her voice sounding, for a moment, just a little too deep and serious '… the final frontier.'

Then she chuckled as she adjusted her safety goggles and, as an extraordinary feeling of speed and strength flowed through the kite and into her and, without even so much as a glance at the pearly blue world behind her, she disappeared, among the stars.

At first they thought Mrs Ockleton was sleeping deeply in her comfortable armchair when they called the next day. No amount of knocking or shouting could wake her though, and she seemed to be in the middle of such a contented and happy dream.

Then they noticed her cold fist holding tightly on to a trailing thread, leading to the brightly coloured ball of wool on the floor, which was lying still at her feet where it had rested, like a kite that had tumbled from the sky.

## Vocabulary

**Filling up**  going to cry

**Ten-foot**  a small alley, an area between houses where garages usually project into and often used by children as a play area – often not more than 'ten-foot' in width

© 2006 Garry Burnett and Crown House Publishing Ltd – *Mrs Ockleton's Rainbow Kite and Other Tales: Thinking Through Literature*

SECTION 1  **Mrs Ockleton's Rainbow Kite**

# 10 Mrs Ockleton's Rainbow Kite

## TEACHERS' NOTES

Pupils will have opportunities to attain at the following Key Stage 3 National Curriculum levels:

## En 2 (Reading)

Pupils will have opportunities to demonstrate reading skills at the following levels:

### At level 5a

a  To show understanding
   Develop inference
   Select appropriate evidence
b  Identify key features, themes and characters
c  Pick out supportive evidence, quotes to support a point of view
d  Understand how texts are organised (and use similar organisational strategies in own work)
e  Compare and contrast texts
f  Discuss the degree of success the author has achieved literary objectives

### At level 6a

g  Read and discuss a wide range of texts
h  Identify *layers* of meaning
i  Identify the effects and significance of texts
j  Express a personal response to texts with reference to language, structure and themes

### At level 7a

k  Select and synthesise information

## En3 (Writing)

Pupils will have opportunities to demonstrate writing skills at the following levels:

### At level 6a

a  To write to engage the reader's interest
b  To use appropriate form and structure

### At level 7a

c  Show clear sense of purpose and audience
d  Express a clear and coherent point of view
e  Write confidently using a range of sentence structures

There are a great many existing examples of the representation of death in contemporary children's culture (largely violent and unpleasant deaths of 'enemies' or evil-doers). I was interested in this story in trying to describe a gentle, positive (if that is possible) experience. For many children their first experience of bereavement is either on a relatively small scale, that of a pet, or with much greater impact and significance, that of a grandparent. Coming to terms with the reality of death is an important rite of passage. One psychologist friend has used the 'Mrs Ockleton' story to help introduce the subject prior to bereavement counselling.

Teacher colleagues have found it helpful to introduce concepts of textual organisation and particularly the 'little clouds' structure of significance in 'beginnings' and 'endings'. The exercises following 'Jack's three wishes' are designed to develop a perspective on story-crafting and interpretation.

The story itself has its origins in two quite disconnected sources: the most important being the experience of the premature and very sad death of a close family friend; by way of contrast, the inspirational music of Gordon Giltrap, particularly 'Rainbow Kites', 'Kaz' and 'On Camber Sands' once again helped me to complete the creative process and allowed the words to surface.

These elements all came together during a very difficult walk on Beverley Westwood, after we had just been given the news that our friend's unsuccessful chemotherapy treatment would be discontinued, leaving little hope for her recovery. On the Westwood was an elderly couple about to fly a large multi-coloured kite. As we watched a strong wind blew and lifted the kite and the lady completely off the ground. The slapstick quality of the situation made me smile and instantly caught my imagination. After that the story then very quickly 'wrote itself'.

Despite the strong rhythmical and musical content to the story there is a deliberately very powerful *visual* dimension to it as well. I vividly imagined many of the scenes before I wrote them down. I remember particularly looking down on the clouds as my wife and I flew back from a weekend in Florence and scribbling on the back of a paper plate 'like mashed potato, great big lumpy mashed potato'.

The recording of the story also owes much to my long-suffering friend Jeff Turner, who is a fabulous source of advice as well as being a technical genius in his studio.

Teachers might like to consider using this story together with the story 'Egging', which deals with similar themes.

This story can be found on Track 5 of the audio CD accompanying this book.

# Mrs Ockleton's Rainbow Kite (1)

1. 'Like a kite which has tumbled from the sky.' 'Mrs Ockleton's Rainbow Kite' ends on this simile. 'Similes' are language devices that writers use when they are describing something by comparing it to something else. One way of thinking about the simile is that it describes 'similarities' between one thing and another, usually in an imaginative and thought-provoking way.

   In 'Mrs Ockleton's Rainbow Kite' there are over 20 similes. Pick out ten that you consider to be effective (that is they do a *good job* at describing).

   a) Write out the simile.

   b) Explain what the simile describes.

   c) Try to explain why you think the writer chose the simile.

   For example:

   a) 'Like a kite, which has tumbled from the sky.'

   b) This simile describes the ball of wool which has fallen from Mrs Ockleton's lap.

   c) The writer possibly chose this simile because he wanted us to connect the experience of Mrs Ockleton's 'dream of flying' with the last thing she saw before she closed her eyes.

2. Imagine 'Mrs Ockleton's Rainbow Kite' is to be made into an animated book and film. You have been invited to submit some designs for scenes from the story. Choose three scenes you would like to illustrate and sketch out designs for them. Use the blank storyboard sheet 'Mrs Ockleton's Rainbow Kite (2)' to present your choices on.

3. The animated film will be backed up by a strong marketing campaign. Design a logo and ideas for merchandise, which will accompany the release of the film. Devise a marketing strategy for the book and film that will promote the story to many different groups of people.

4. In the story there are many mentions of 'media': newspaper headlines, TV and radio coverage. Research some of the stories mentioned in the text (plane-spotters in Athens, Ken Livingstone and the pigeons of Trafalgar Square and so on). Can you find possible sources for some of the stories? Write a 'reader's guide to Mrs Ockleton's Rainbow Kite'.

5. How would future readers be able to guess that this was a story written in 2002?

6. Design and write one of the newspaper front pages detailing Mrs Ockleton's adventure; for example, 'UFO – Unbelievable Flying Ockleton', the 'Spot the Difference' competition headline.

7. There are two other stories mentioned in 'Mrs Ockleton' that have yet to be written (and they will be!): 'Mrs Ockleton and the Hair-styling Helmet Charade' and 'Mrs Ockleton and the Amazing Pre-programmable Dancing Shoes Fiasco'. Using these titles and, in keeping with the style of the original story, write out your ideas for one of these 'prequels'.

8. The music of the celebrated guitarist Gordon Giltrap inspired the story 'Mrs Ockleton's Rainbow Kite'. Read Gordon's notes on music and stories printed in the Foreword.

9. When you listen to 'Mrs Ockleton's Rainbow Kite' how important do you think the music is in creating atmosphere? Comment particularly on the use of the three tunes and their use in 'Mrs Ockleton's Rainbow Kite'.

10. Write or set to music a story in which music plays an important part. If it is possible, use technology to record your story with the music. Play these to the class.

# Mrs Ockleton's Rainbow Kite (2)

| Image | Words |
|-------|-------|
|       |       |
|       |       |
|       |       |
|       |       |
|       |       |
|       |       |
|       |       |

© 2006 Garry Burnett and Crown House Publishing Ltd – *Mrs Ockleton's Rainbow Kite and Other Tales: Thinking Through Literature*

# Beginnings and endings of stories

Read the following story and then from the designated point try to *predict how* the story will end.

## Jack's three wishes

Once upon a time long ago, a poor woodcutter called Jack was making his way home from work through the forest when he heard a tiny voice calling from the edge of the path near his feet.

'Help, help,' his little voice squeaked. 'Quickly, look down here.'

Jack looked down and to his amazement saw a tiny man, no taller than a dandelion struggling to release his foot that had become trapped in the tangled roots of a great oak tree.

Although he was hurrying home because he was late and his wife would worry, Jack took his axe and raised it to hack away at the roots.

'Hurry,' said the little man. 'If I don't get back below ground before sunset, I shall be trapped here forever!'

In a few seconds Jack had hacked his way through the thick tree roots and the little man gratefully rubbed his sore ankle.

'Thank you sir,' he said. 'Thank you very much. Now I must go, but listen carefully as I have something very important to say. If you return to this very spot an hour before sunset tomorrow, I will grant you one wish, which may be for whatever you choose.'

And then he vanished behind a dock leaf before you could say 'must dash'.

Well! Jack rushed home to tell his wife and elderly parents the wonderful news. He called them all in to sit around the old pine kitchen table in the tumble-down cottage they shared, to tell the story of the meeting with the tiny green man and the promise of a wish he had been given.

It was Jack's wife who spoke first.

'Jack,' she said, 'Although we have been married for ten years, we have not yet been blessed with a child. And now the doctor says it looks unlikely that we will ever be so. Use your wish to make our lives complete. Wish for a child.'

'Jack,' said Jack's mother, who was very old. 'You are my only son. I cared for you through all kinds of illness. Now my sight is starting to fail and within a few months it seems I shall be completely blind. Use your wish to restore my sight. I would hate to be a burden to you the short time I have left. Please let me die happy. Let me keep my sight.'

'Bah,' said Jack's father, who was known to be a practical man. 'We are poor. Last winter we nearly starved. We cannot afford another mouth to feed and you certainly shouldn't be wasting your wish on old folks like us who might only be here for a short while longer. Wish for riches Jack, wish for money. Let us live our lives in comfort, not scratching out a living in poverty and desperation.'

Poor Jack was troubled and confused so he lit a candle and stayed awake all night to think.

GARRY BURNETT
(*adapted from a traditional tale*)

Now write down your prediction for the end of the story.

_____

_____

_____

_____

_____

_____

_____

_____

_____

_____

© 2006 Garry Burnett and Crown House Publishing Ltd – *Mrs Ockleton's Rainbow Kite and Other Tales: Thinking Through Literature*

SECTION 1 | **Mrs Ockleton's Rainbow Kite**

# Beginnings and endings of stories (contd.)

> *One possible ending to the story!*
> The next day at the appointed hour Jack stood quietly under the great oak tree waiting for the little man to appear and, true to his elfish word, he was there waiting to meet Jack .
>   'Well, Jack. Have you made a decision? What do you wish for?'
>   'Yes. I would like my mother to see my child, in a cradle made of gold, encrusted with diamonds.'
>   'A wise decision Jack,' said the little man, his dark eyes shining like conkers. 'Your wish is my command.'

With 'hindsight' (looking back at something) it is easy to see how the three elements 'connect' and to guess what the 'answer' was.
How did your 'predicted ending' compare to the actual ending?

## Further activities

When Garry Burnett wrote the story 'Mrs Ockleton's Rainbow Kite' he used a structuring method sometimes called 'little clouds'. That is, he included at the beginning of the story, details that seem to be unimportant but grow in importance (like approaching clouds).

- Analyse the *beginning* and *ending* of 'Mrs Ockleton's Rainbow Kite'.
- What connections can you see there between them?
- Are there any details that appear to be relatively insignificant at first?
- Apply this method of analysis to other stories in the collection; for example, 'A Yuletide Tale'.

## ✏ Write

Write a story using the 'little clouds' method of connecting beginnings and endings of stories.

> **Notes**

© 2006 Garry Burnett and Crown House Publishing Ltd – *Mrs Ockleton's Rainbow Kite and Other Tales: Thinking Through Literature*

# Dealing with difficult emotional issues raised by the story

## Bereavement and grief

There cannot be any more traumatic, life-changing or emotionally disturbing event than the death of a loved one. Although the event could be fraught with upsetting and bewildering issues for a young person, the experience can serve as an important induction into the reality of life and the inevitability of death for all of us. For many children the first experience of this is the death of a grandparent and the way they cope with this experience can differ tremendously from the responses of adults around them.

The story 'Mrs Ockleton's Rainbow Kite' was born out of this very experience and was an attempt, in writing, to come to terms with the reality of death in an optimistic way. I was quite moved by the symbolism of the unfettered kite (which in some cultures signifies the soul 'taking flight') and the double image of the grounded kite and the rainbow-coloured ball of wool being connected in the imagination. At the time of writing the story I was also very moved by the death of the singer Eva Cassidy, who in her astonishing version of 'Over the Rainbow' (connected very much to the story 'Mrs Ockleton') appears to be singing her own lament. Similarly, David Bowie's haunting rendition of Jacques Brel's 'My Death' is probably the single most influential lyric to a song I have ever heard and seemed to me to present a totally unsentimental, mystical insight into the issue.

The story can open up extremely sensitive areas for teachers and children to talk about, write about and explore. I hope that these brief notes and suggested activities provide some guidance and insights to help readers to possibly use the story as a way of introducing certain issues and allowing some of the thoughts and feelings a child could have to surface in what will ultimately be a positive way.

## Coming to terms with loss

The psychologist Elisabeth Kubler-Ross claimed that there were several significant phases of mourning.

**Shock** usually associated with the initial stages of grief – feelings include those of loss and disbelief.
**Denial** relates to the impulse to protest or display anger about the death 'I can't believe this' or 'This can't have happened to me' are common phrases associated with this stage.
**Anger** relates to the apparently irrational and extreme feelings of anger towards the deceased person or towards themselves ('If only I had said or done').
**Bargaining** characterised by the belief that by performing certain ritualistic actions some semi-magical remedy will occur ('If I promise to do this …').
**Despair** a stage of desolate realisation that the situation cannot be changed – a dangerous time when clinical depression and the risk of suicide is at its greatest.
**Acceptance** this stage is reached when the bereaved person can begin to accept the loss and make positive steps to move on with their life, not forgetting the deceased person but now able to cope by not being overwhelmed by grief and in a position to be able to form new relationships.

Alexandra Kennedy in her book *Losing a Parent* (1991, HarperCollins) suggests that there are at least ten important steps involved in reaching the stage of 'acceptance' and in coming to terms with the loss of a loved one:

1. Acknowledge the importance and power of the event.
2. Take time each day to silently contemplate your grief.
3. Address any unfinished business.
4. Start to create new family patterns, especially for important calendar events like Christmas, holidays, birthdays and so on.
5. Monitor the quality of your own life.
6. Don't be too anxious to 'get back to normal'.
7. Explore ways to fulfil the role the deceased person has left.
8. Rely on friends and people who offer help (don't just say 'thanks' and ignore offers of support).
9. Commemorate the event each year.
10. Look at the changes the event has brought to your life in a positive way.

## Responses

A child's response to an event could seem in some cases to be shallow and even disinterested. The child may say what are considered to be inappropriate things or appear to be preoccupied with matters disconnected with the loss. It is important to realise that grief for the child could materialise in all sorts of ways over a period of many years when that loved one is missing from important family events and special occasions. It could be that in private moments when they recall their lost loved one the emotions begin to surface most powerfully.

This grief could materialise in:

- certain forms of *anxiety* (anger, depression, worries)
- *physical* ways (sleep loss, eating disorders or even symptoms which appear to mimic the deceased person's condition)
- *emotional* ways (tearfulness, distractedness)
- *sociability* (strains on friendships, school, work).

There is no one uniform, predictable or indeed 'correct' way to respond to death but there are things that we can do to support the important process of grieving.

In Malet Lambert School Language College the story 'Mrs Ockleton's Rainbow Kite' has been used most effectively with groups of Year 9 pupils who have written poetry (an effective and popular method of ventilating strong feelings of grief) inspired by the story and connecting to their own personal experiences of loss.

Developing 'self-awareness' is an important quality of emotional intelligence. Here are some suggested ways that the teacher can support a grieving child:

1 Acknowledge that the impact on the child could cause depths of pain that are yet to be revealed.

2 Learn about the different emotional manifestations of grief: disbelief, numbness, shock, anxiety, fear, guilt, anger and so on.

3 Smile, be positive and do not in any way treat the child as if 'there is something wrong' with them.

4 Try not to take a child's rejection or negativity personally.

5 Help in small ways, contact the child's parents or carers to share information and monitor behaviour.

6 Don't be surprised if a child suddenly changes the subject in the middle of a conversation. Go with them and talk about what they want to discuss. You should not expect instant results.

7 Don't be afraid to say 'I don't know'.

8 If you find the subject difficult, don't be afraid to say so – that very fact may help a child with coming to terms with their own feelings.

## Six activities that may help in coming to terms with grief

### 1 Treasure chest activity

A child could collate a treasure chest of memorabilia connected with the deceased person and create an inventory, explaining why the artifact is of particular importance to the memory of their loved one.

### 2 Letter to a loved one

It is sometimes useful to write a letter to the loved one in order to reconnect with them after they have died. Some things that a child could include in their letter are:

- What has happened since the loved one's death – tell them about it.
- What the child misses about them.
- What regrets the child has about things about which have remained undone.
- What the child really appreciated about the loved one.
- How the child wants to remember them.

### 3 Create a special place – sanctuary

A child could create a special room, or corner or area of the garden where they can go to remember the person they loved. Perhaps they could design what they want the area to look like – which flowers, ornaments, photographs they would like to preserve there.

### 4 Using 'Mrs Ockleton's Rainbow Kite'

*Emotional responses*

How did the child *feel* about the ending of the story? Did they find it connects with their own experience in any way? Ask them to write down the various feelings they have about the events in the story.

*Respond in verse*

The child could write down a poetic response based on the language and events of the story – perhaps use 'found' poetry techniques.

*Write a letter to the author*

The author would be delighted to hear from people who have read and been affected by the story in any way. Did the story help the child to cope with their situation? How? You can contact him via www.garryburnett.com.

## 5 Write a ten-page book dedicated to the loved one

Page titles for the book could include:

1. Cover design including the name of the loved one.
2. Good things the child remembers about the relationship.
3. Words and phrases the child remembers them saying.
4. Things the child wishes could have happened.
5. Angry feelings the child has about them now.
6. What mattered to the child in the relationship.
7. A request for the loved one.
8. A wish for the loved one.
9. An ending for the book – saying goodbye.
10. Back cover.

## 6 Create a lifeline

This activity can be useful in helping to balance the positive and negative events of life when the overwhelming feeling is that of negativity. The lifeline can be given values in terms of the impact of the event on the person in relation to others.

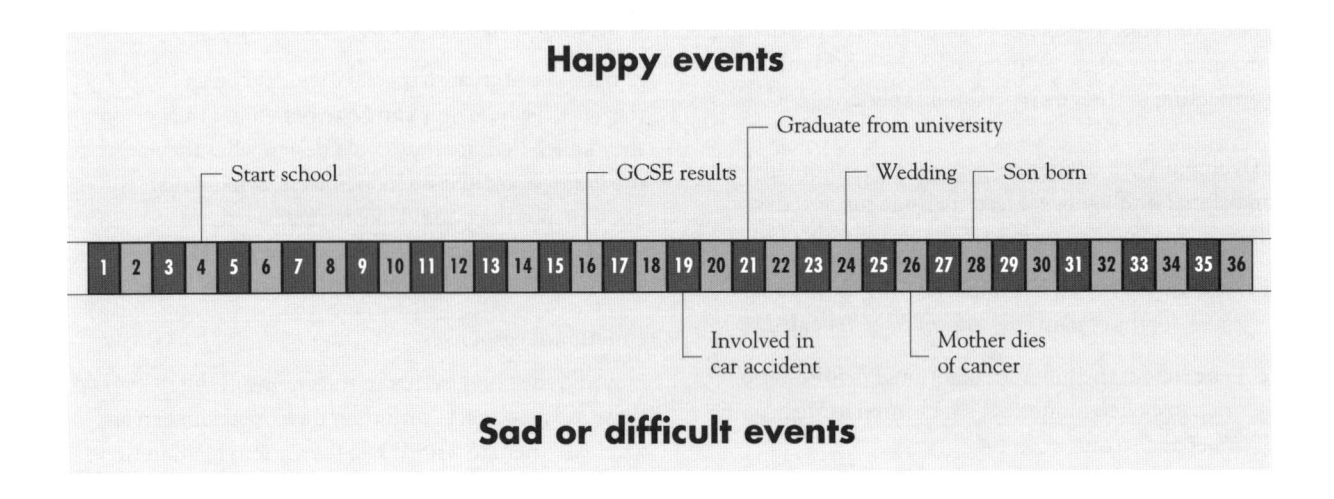

**Happy events**

Start school — GCSE results — Graduate from university — Wedding — Son born

1 2 3 4 5 6 7 8 9 10 11 12 13 14 15 16 17 18 19 20 21 22 23 24 25 26 27 28 29 30 31 32 33 34 35 36

Involved in car accident — Mother dies of cancer

**Sad or difficult events**

# Further Guidelines

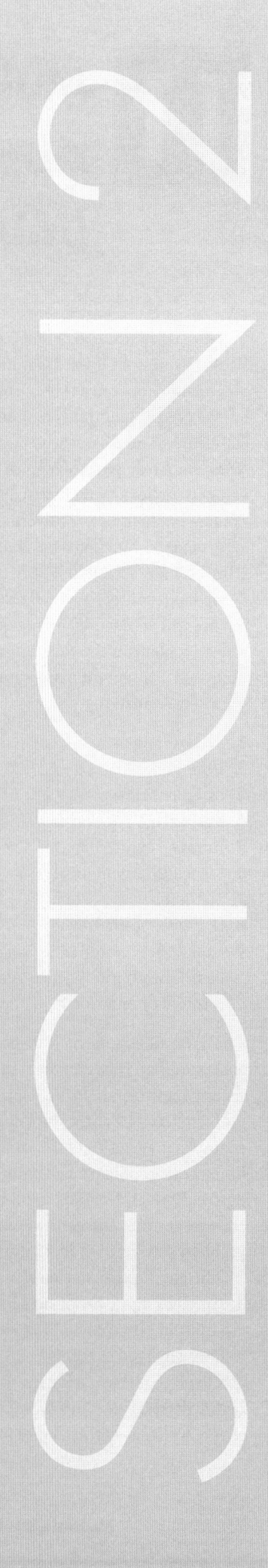

**SECTION 2**

# 11 Multiple Intelligence Approaches to Reading Texts (MIARTS)

In his world famous book *Frames of Mind* (1983, Basic Books) Professor Howard Gardner of Harvard University proposed a theory of how intelligence might be observed in manifold or 'multiple' ways. Gardner claimed that intelligence is broadly demonstrated when we attempt to solve problems or construct things of value to the society we live in. Naturally this has wide-ranging implications considering the diverse talents, achievements and potential of a multi-cultural, multi-ethnic society such as our own.

He has recently suggested that in 'perceiving or representing the world around us' and in the way we 'solve problems and make things of value to the society we live in', this might manifest in eight or more different ways. These are:

1 Verbal/Linguistic
2 Visual/Spatial
3 Interpersonal
4 Musical
5 Intrapersonal
6 Logical/Mathematical
7 Naturalist
8 Bodily/Kinesthetic
9 Existential (Gardner has suggested that there might be this ninth intelligence relating to philosophical, spiritual orientation)

These 'intelligences' have no particular hierarchy except in their relative worth to the living culture or society they operate in. A 'logical-mathematical' problem faced by a stockbroker working in the City, for example, may not be of the same character as a bodily-kinesthetic problem faced by an Amazon Rainforest native. Both endeavours could be valued equally in their cultural context and generate equal levels of intelligent problem-solving in order to reach a solution.

This more expansive view of intelligence is now accepted by many people in education as being among the most important thinking about the way that we *learn* to have emerged in recent years.

Given that there are many different ways human beings demonstrate 'intelligence', should it not follow that teachers design activities in order to reflect this? In the case of reading and responding to imaginative fiction this could especially be so.

The following pages contain a wide selection of suggestions for activities to promote thoughtful, active reading using this range of intelligences, all of which could be incorporated into a structured reading experience.

## Reading MIARTS – some practical approaches

### 1 Verbal/Linguistic

This dimension of intelligence is particularly aligned to all the complex thinking, conceptual patterning and interaction that we create through the spoken and written word and is 'awakened' by many varied activities involving language processing and reflection. For example, in activities involving: responses to literature, including exposition, comprehension and prediction; contact with narrative in other forms, including film, speech, drama and poetry; debates, discussions, expression of ideas; understanding of figurative and ironic uses of language, experimentation with vocabulary, etymology, register, creative and discursive writing for different audiences and purposes, diaries, monologues, self-talk, self-evaluation and so on.

In responding to texts we can develop this intelligence by:

- Altering genre/register/audience transformation (e.g., turn the text into a radio broadcast, news bulletin, diary entry, children's story, short story, poem, play, mini-saga letter).
- Re-write the text as if from a different character's point of view (e.g., 'The Three Little Pigs' from the wolf's point of view).
- Write a 'beginner's guide to …' pamphlet on the topic or text using written information and diagrams.
- Writing spoof versions of the text, parodying the style, subject matter or characters.
- Finding examples of apocryphal, parallel texts (e.g., poetry written about the same subject, in the same era, or different genres such as Pepys account of 'The Great Fire', Defoe's 'Journal of the Plague Year', Melville and whaling).

- Reducing the text to its bare minimum while retaining the meaning (word-process a section of text that has to be reduced in order to retain meaning using the least number of words).
- Making an *abridged* version of the text for a different audience.
- Substituting key words in the text with others (less appropriate, incongruous, dramatic and so on) and encourage pupils to guess which words have been replaced and why.
- Investigating different drafts or different translations. Analysing the differences and exploring the reasons for decisions made by the writers (e.g., translations of Chaucer).
- Predicting – producing a write-on (e.g., in 'Our Day Out' what happens next?).
- Allowing pupils to create word-puzzles, crosswords, quizzes, games connected with the vocabulary of the text.
- Playing 'Mastermind' or 'Who wants to be a Millionaire' in order to inject fun and challenge into remembering detailed information about the text (see *Learning to Learn: Making Learning Work For All Students*, Burnett, 2002, Crown House Publishing Ltd).
- Inventing conversations between characters in different texts – imagine Macbeth and Henry V in conversation, or Beowulf and Sir Gawain.
- Putting characters onto TV game shows (imagine Uncle Kevin on 'Blind Date', or a 'Big Brother' house composed of literary, or even exclusively Shakespearian characters). Write the script of an imagined episode.

## 2 Visual/Spatial

The key feature of this intelligence is the ability to visualise images and objects, to represent things in visual terms using non-verbal organisational, graphic and diagrammatic systems such as concept-mapping and mind-mapping. The ability to imagine scenes and environments, estimate in terms of spatial relationship and to respond to imagery is closely linked to this intelligence.

In responding to texts we can develop this intelligence by:

- Making flow diagrams to represent sequences of events.
- Making mind-maps, clockwise- and concept-maps to represent and embellish the 'big picture', connecting ideas together.
- Using a digital camera to produce 'PowerPoint' slide shows, using models and toys to make stories, poem illustrations and so on.
- Producing cartoon/illustrated versions of the text (no words allowed).
- Reducing the text into key 'symbols' and motifs for recall. Draw them on to cards.
- Finding and using paintings that depict aspects of the topic or era (e.g., medieval life, theatre, warfare).
- Creating a document file of relevant photographs to support or illustrate the text (taken from internet/Encarta and so on).
- Imagining turning the text into a short film or documentary. Storyboarding a sequence of images to film that will represent the text (see storyboard on resource on pages 73, 90 and 103).
- Making maps to represent the geographical/topographical sequence of events (historical/literary – see Hardy's Wessex, Tolkien's Middle Earth).
- Watching documentary or dramatic versions of the text (e.g., Shakespeare or a novelisation or filmed historical/biographical event). Write about insertions, composition, set, props, design, alterations, omissions and so on.
- Practising internal visualisation – 'time travel' to places and events connected with the text, role-play imaginary telephone conversations between characters or key figures involved in your text.
- Imagining *being* a character and doing a 'walk through' of the text (location, décor, surroundings and so on). Write a description of the scene the character sees.
- Making posters to encapsulate key ideas, illustrate scenes and so on.
- Producing 3D models out of 'plasticine' or clay (e.g., Tennyson's 'Charge of the Light Brigade', the storming of Dunsinane Castle in *Macbeth*, the balcony scene in *Romeo and Juliet*).
- Annotating the written text with symbols/colours to represent moods and concepts.
- Producing a mural/collage to represent the episode or theme, story, poem and so on.
- Producing visual graphs that tabulate key information in the text (appearances, participation, mentions).
- Making Powerpoint slide shows using digital photography to represent narrative, synopsis and so on.
- Designing book covers and promotional material for new editions or for marketing campaigns.
- Looking for ways of representing the 'big picture' of the story in visual terms.

## 3 Interpersonal

This form of intelligence is integrally bound with communication skills and language and also relates very closely to emotional and personal development (see particularly the activities relating to 'A Yuletide Tale').

**Multiple Intelligence Approaches to Reading Texts (MIARTS)**

It involves the capacity to be 'mindful' of others, to exercise appropriate registers and empathy and to anticipate the needs and reactions of others in order to communicate effectively. This intelligence might be developed through experiential drama, role-play, group work, simulations relating to people situations. It might also be developed through looking at verbal and non-verbal cues in communication, work on language acquisition and by teaching others.

In responding to texts we can develop this intelligence by:

- Role-playing 'scenes' from the text, script or improvising missing scenes.
- Dramatising meetings between literary figures.
- Imagining you are invited to be a guest lecturer/opening conference speaker on the writer studied. Prepare a five-minute introduction with illustrations (possible use of PowerPoint/OHT/interactive whiteboard).
- 'Hot seating' a character – (or) by the teacher being the character and the pupils interrogating them.
- Acting out a representation of the text (e.g., Reduced Shakespeare's five-minute *Romeo and Juliet*).
- Predicting – anticipate the responses of people, write them out in short dramatic form.
- Making 'push plays' (two people sitting next to each other silently write to each other 'pushing' a piece of paper to and fro in order to respond).
- 'Jigsawing' the text (different groups read different pieces of information, one person has to become an 'expert' and to report their findings to another group).
- Exploring the representation of people skills in characters (e.g., Tom in *Four Weddings*, Uncle Kevin anywhere!).
- Preparing a 'Big Read'-style advocacy script for a book of your choice. Video record it!

## 4 Musical

Through this intelligence we become conscious of 'rhythmic and tonal patterns', sensitive to the influence of the human voice, natural sounds and musical instruments. It is about 'timing', pace and metre and can influence the syllabic construction of poetry or the grammatical, syntactical structure of speech or descriptive prose. In the descriptive phrase beginning 'the "sloe-black", slow, black, fishing boat-bobbing sea' taken from *Under Milk Wood* for example, Dylan Thomas demonstrates a mastery of rhythmical, musical language. Early learning is made more dynamically effective by the use of music and songs, where children develop awareness of structured rhythmical patterns, rhythms and beats. Listening to ideas expressed in songs, singing, humming, tapping fingers or pencils, chanting or rapping; being aware or being affected by bird song, the sounds of the sea and sounds of nature are all signs of our musical intelligence surfacing.

In responding to texts we can develop this intelligence by:

- Finding and playing music composed to represent the theme you are exploring.
- Setting the reading of your text to appropriate music (listen to 'Mrs Ockleton's Rainbow Kite' on the accompanying CD and discuss the use of background music).
- Searching for folk-songs, lyrics and atmospheric tunes to enhance the study of the topic (see John Schlesinger's adaptation of *Far from the Madding Crowd*).
- Turning the information in the text into a 'ballad' (e.g., 'The Ballad of Rhoda Brook', 'The Ballad of Macbeth', 'The Song of the Gladiator').
- Turning information into lyrics 'to be sung to the tune of …' (e.g., the *National Anthem*).
- Experimenting with reading the text aloud at different speeds. Demarcate the text with auditory cues (emphasis, tone of voice, speed, pause and so on).
- Using a metronome/karaoke/drum-machine to turn ideas into a 'rap' or song.
- Studying lyrics from different eras that represent different themes.
- Looking at musical theatre versions of texts *Oliver*, *Les Miserables* and so on. Write songs for new musical adaptations (e.g., 'Tom's Blues' in *To Kill a Mockingbird*).

## 5 Intrapersonal

This form of intelligence manifests in our ability to philosophise about our personal identity and self-hood and involves increasing self-consciousness and meditative reflection relating to moral, spiritual and ethical matters. It is also about the 'personal' response to and perception of the world around us and reflects individual, private traits and characteristics.

In responding to texts we can develop this intelligence by:

- Questioning – list questions to ask a key person/expert associated with the text.
- Writing down twenty 'answers' based on the text. Work out what the questions might be using the text as a basis for enquiry.
- Writing diary entries for key personalities mentioned in the text.
- Turning extracts from texts into 'first person', altering the syntax and vocabulary appropriately and experimenting with changes in meaning thrown up by the alteration of viewpoint.

- Writing evaluations of what has been gained *personally* from the study of this text.
- Recording personal emotional responses to the text. Record these feelings by annotating the text appropriately.
- Assessing the spiritual implications of our personal response to the story. Does it connect to our faith or beliefs about God, existence and ourselves in any way?

## 6 Logical/Mathematical

This area is most often associated with scientific, linear and mathematical 'Socratic' thinking and is reflected in the ability to draw conclusions based on analysis of cause and effect, and to hypothesise and plan systematically in order to give substantial and pertinent answers to problems.

In responding to texts we can develop this intelligence by:

- Sequencing – photocopying and cutting up texts into sections for rearranging following exploratory talk (see 'The Mariner's Tale' section).
- Sectionalising – creating sub-headings. White out headings or sub-headings and so on and re-invent them, also try chapter titles and so on.
- Experimenting with deletion of key words (cloze test).
- Designing board games that use the text as its inspiration (e.g., *To Kill a Mockingbird*, *I'm the King of the Castle*).
- 'Categorising' ideas – is it possible to chunk certain themes or aspect of the text into categories or sections? Make revision cards with key 'topics' or categories.
- Creating a set of arguments 'for and against' something the text represents. (Was Richard III a good king? Could Macbeth's downfall have been prevented?) Write these arguments in columns of opposing views.
- Writing study guides, 'recipes', 'instruction sheets' or 'good guides to' incorporating simplified synopsis of the text.
- Creating chronological versions of the text (first … then … then …). Write them up on to cards and experiment with re-ordering information.
- Rank-ordering/prioritising ideas in the text (most to least important, depending on content and viewpoint taken).
- Grouping connected ideas into patterns – experiment with grouping and categorisation.
- Using Venn diagrams to represent different associated ideas in the text.

## 7 Naturalist

We all know individuals who seem to have a special affinity with Nature; they might be good gardeners, meteorologists, farmers or growers, or perhaps they have a passion for cosmology or astronomy, geography or for breeding animals and birds. This is Gardner's 'Naturalist' intelligence, reflected in knowledge of the Earth, the natural world and its rhythms and shown by those who are attuned to it.

In responding to texts we can develop this intelligence by:

- Playing sounds from nature to accompany and enhance the learning.
- Visiting the environment/setting of the text.
- Being aware of topographical descriptions in the text, weather and geography – the use of 'sympathetic' background in literary and dramatic texts.
- Charting the depiction of animals and the representation of the relationship between man and animals in the text.
- Exploring natural allusions through characters' names, place names and so on (e.g., Gabriel Oak, *Far From The Madding Crowd*; Heathcliff, *Wuthering Heights*).

## 8 Bodily/Kinesthetic

The intelligence connected with 'doing' something 'physical', that is, the manipulation of self, objects or environment in such a way as to solve problems, make representations of the world and produce artefacts of value. Intellectual chauvinism and the emphasis on testing through language and number has too often relegated this intelligence to a position of perceived inferiority, and yet many of our culture's proudest achievements have come from the artists, actors or sportsmen who can physically manipulate objects or themselves in space and time in order to produce virtuous expressions of creativity and endeavour.

In responding to texts we can develop this intelligence by:

- Creating 'tableaux' or a gallery of sculptures representing different stages in the text (i.e. the pupils in groups produce the 'statues').
- Miming key aspects of the text, play 'Give Us A Clue' with answers or vocabulary related to the topic read.
- Planning and producing a video documentary on the subject of the text (multiple intelligence activity). See examples such as the BBC 'shorts'.
- Viewing/studying/producing dance representations of stories and themes.
- Working out a movement game or routine based on the text.
- Creating dramas/sketches representing aspects of the text.

- Dressing up as characters from the text and having a 'theme' day/lesson (e.g., a 'Chaucer' evening, serving appropriate food, creating entertainment).
- Playing 'run-around' – making 'people graphs' to see 'who agrees with…' and so on.
- Researching and becoming experts in groups on a particular aspect of the topic or text. Prepare presentations to the class about findings.
- Visiting!

## 9 Existential

Gardner has suggested that this intelligence could be closely related to 'intrapersonal' intelligence and is displayed in the spiritual, philosophical and moral depth of thought. It involves the exploration of profound and universal issues such as existence and God, Time and Being and is reflected in the rituals and beliefs the individual pursues, including religious faith.

In responding to texts we can develop this intelligence by:

- Assessing the spiritual implications of personal responses. Does it connect to faith or beliefs about self, God and existence in any way?
- Exploring 'big' questions posed by the text – moral/spiritual/personal and so on.
- Exploring questions of 'self' and identity in the text (e.g., Macbeth, Hamlet).
- Writing diaries, confessionals, prayers for key characters.

# 12 Anderson's Revised Taxonomy

Anderson's revised taxonomy proposes the following ladder of thinking skills – the first step of the ladder, remembering quantities of knowledge and facts, is the least sophisticated in terms of cognitive challenge. Hopefully this will provide a useful matrix for colleagues wishing to construct their own questions and activities or to develop further the responses they have achieved so far.

## 1 REMEMBERING

*Recognise, list, describe, identify, retrieve, name …*

Can the pupil RECALL information?

Typical questions/activities might include:

*What happened? How many? What is? Describe what happened? Who said? Identify who?*

## 2 UNDERSTANDING

*Interpret, exemplify, summarise, infer, paraphrase …*

Can the pupil EXPLAIN ideas or concepts?

Typical questions/activities might include:

*Explain why … Clarify the … What do you think could have happened next? What was the main idea?*

## 3 APPLYING

*Implement, carry out, use …*

Can the pupil USE the new knowledge in another familiar situation?

Typical questions/activities might include:

*Put into your own words … Use this information to … Try yourself …*

## 4 ANALYSING

*Compare, contrast, attribute, organise, deconstruct …*

Can the pupil DIFFERENTIATE between constituent parts?

Typical questions/activities might include:

*How is … similar to …? Why did x occur? What were some of the motives behind …? If x had happened, what might the ending have been? Can you distinguish between …? Why did the …?*

## 5 EVALUATING

*Check, critique, judge, hypothesise …*

Can the pupil JUSTIFY a decision or course of action?

Typical questions/activities might include:

*Could there have been a better solution to …? What do you think about …? How effective is …? What would you recommend? How well …?*

## 6 CREATING

*Design, construct, plan, produce …*

Can the pupil GENERATE new products, ideas or ways of viewing things?

Typical questions/activities might include:

*Can you design …? Write your own … Produce a …*